$urvive the
Great Inflation

$urvive the Great Inflation

How to Protect Your Family, Your Future and Your Fortune from the Worst Fed Regime Ever

Michael Murphy, CFA

Editor, *New World Investor*

This publication is designed to provide accurate and authoritative information in regard to the subject matter covered. It is sold with the understanding that neither the author nor the publisher are engaged in rendering investment, accounting, legal or other professional service or advice. If investment advice or other expert assistance is required, the services of an independent professional should be sought.

ISBN 978-0-9788-7500-8

LCCN: 2010939065

Cataloging Information:

BISAC Subjects

BUS031000 BUSINESS & ECONOMICS / Inflation
BUS036000 BUSINESS & ECONOMICS / Investments & Securities
BUS050020 BUSINESS & ECONOMICS / Personal Finance / Investing
BUS050030 BUSINESS & ECONOMICS / Personal Finance / Money
    Management
BUS050040 BUSINESS & ECONOMICS / Personal Finance / Retirement
    Planning

Library of Congress Subject Headings

Inflation
Investing
Personal Finance
Retirement Planning
Hyperinflation
Gold
Stocks

Dedicated to my family

"country folks can survive"

Table of Contents

Part V: What Our Country Could Do – But Won't

Acknowledgments

My thanks to the *New World Investor* subscribers who post comments and questions daily to explore new ideas and challenge my thinking. Thanks to Ghislain Viau for the beautiful covers and book design, to Laren Bright for the cover copy and subtitle, and to Tina Lo Sasso for launching the book. Many people read, commented or edited various stages of this book and I want to thank them all, especially Dan Murray, for the numerous improvements they wrought.

Introduction

Honesty is the best policy.
—Benjamin Franklin

his is a book about simple, obvious things that apparently are hidden in plain sight, and The Powers That Be who either can't or won't see them. As a result, high-level decisions are being made and actions taken that will have disastrous consequences for our country, our lives and our portfolios if you do not take evasive action immediately.

The U.S. economy is in the grip of three powerful deflationary forces

The first is deleveraging and the credit bust. Everyone sees this one, but few realize there is a powerful generational driver behind it that will not respond to fiscal stimulus, monetary expansion, cheerleading or any other of the arrows in the government's quiver.

The second powerful deflationary force is demographics – the aging and retirement of the baby boomers. For some reason, little attention is paid to this one either, even though the numbers are obvious and huge. And again, this demographic driver will not respond to government tinkering with the macro, top-down economy.

The third powerful deflationary force, which no one seems to see except me and, now, you, is the accelerating spread of technology. Moore's Law that implies semiconductor costs fall 50% every 24 months is now riding on the Internet Protocol over fiberoptic lines and microwave transmissions to every corner of the world. Rapidly falling costs = rapidly falling prices = deflation.

So should you position yourself for a serious deflation – Great Depression II – the Dow 1000 scenario the Elliott Wave gurus threaten us with? No. Is it really time to get guns, gold and gardens? Maybe, but not because we are going into a deflationary downward spiral.

One powerful inflationary force

We are not going into a downward spiral because these three deflationary forces are up against a far more powerful counter-vailing force: Fed Chairman Ben Bernanke. He is an expert on the Great Depression, he wrote his thesis on it, he taught it, and he has every intention of avoiding Great Depression II on his watch at the Fed. He also has the tools to avoid it. You may think, as I do, that it would be better to be the willow tree that bends in this deflationary storm, to ride it out. But Bernanke has chosen – *had* to choose, given his background – the way of the oak. Stand tall, be strong, be rigid, don't give an inch to the storm and there's a 99% chance you'll survive. Which leaves a 1% chance we lose the whole country.

Those are the percentages in his mind, because he only sees the credit deleveraging part of the storm. Demographics and tech-nology have not crossed his mind, although they are up front in this book. And they make the odds of the oak still standing some-thing closer to 70% than 99%. As Bernanke applies his powerful, inappropriate tools to avoiding Great Depression II, there is a 70% chance he is going to cause the Great Inflation.

There is a 30% chance he will make a misstep or be blindsided by demographics and technology, and cause a Hyperinflation. In a Hyperinflation, society breaks down. No one will accept the currency. The stores empty of food. Wives prostitute themselves in return for canned goods and stored grains. Husbands band together to protect what they have, or to go take things from others. Children work all day long collecting cardboard, scrap metal and edible plants. The unlucky mix vegetable oil with dirt and fry dirt cakes just to stop the hunger pangs. All of these things have happened in the past as a currency collapsed, and a currency goes from accepted to collapsed in a matter of weeks. It can happen here.

Either the Great Inflation or a Hyperinflation might be followed by Great Depression II sometime in the future, but Bernanke will be long gone from the Fed by then.

I wrote this book to reveal the true deflationary forces to you, describe the inevitable Bernanke response and tell you how to monitor this epic battle and position yourself to Survive the Great Inflation. Actually, to thrive in the Great Inflation, or even a Hyperinflation, or whatever it turns out to be. It is going to be brutal. You, your family, and your friends who will listen are going to come out of this just fine.

Time is short; let's get started.

PART I

The Issues

If a man empties his purse into his head, no
man can take it away from him. An investment
in knowledge always pays the best interest.
—Benjamin Franklin

CHAPTER 1

Deflation or Inflation?

Being ignorant is not so much a shame,
as being unwilling to learn.

—Benjamin Franklin

What will be the biggest factor in your investment returns for the next five years? It will be whether the United States is about to enter a depression/deflation or an inflation, possibly a hyperinflation. The story of the decade through 2009 was dollar depreciation due to the persistent inflation in the US. Indeed the story of the last 70 years has been dollar depreciation, again driven by inflation. This was inflation in the classical sense of an increasing money supply racing ahead of the increase in physical production. Prices generally rose during this time, sometimes faster, sometimes slower. And the government measures of inflation also increased, but at different rates depending on both what prices were doing and on how heavily the statistics were manipulated. Figure 1 shows the dollar's foreign exchange loss over a period of 39 years, from 1971 when the United States left the gold standard through the end of 2007 (See chart on next page).

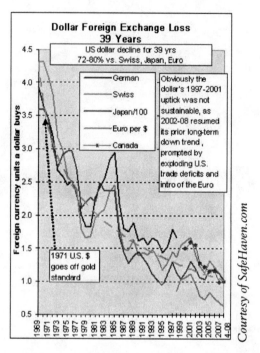

Courtesy of SafeHaven.com

The dollar can be weak against other currencies, or against a basket of commodities (which we call inflation), or both. The question is: Why was the dollar so weak during this long stretch? As you can see from Figure 2, in the mid-90s the Federal Reserve, led by Alan Greenspan, made an obvious decision to dramatically increase the rate of growth in our money supply.

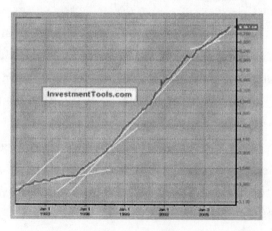

Although Treasury secretaries continued to chant their mantra that the U. S. was committed to a strong dollar policy, it is obvious from Figure 2 that their real commitment was to pumping out enough money to keep the good times rolling in the US. This policy change led to a series of bubbles in Internet stocks, real estate, consumer credit, and ultimately Treasury bonds that have had a dramatic effect on both the real and financial economies of the entire world.

In the future, the dollar will be a good measure of whether the US is in deflation or inflation. If the deflationists are correct, commodities will continue to fall in terms of the US dollar, and it would be reasonable to expect to see dollar strength against the euro, yen and other occurrences. If the inflationists are correct, commodity prices will rise and the dollar will be weak against the Chinese yuan, Australian and Canadian dollars.

The reason the deflation/inflation debate is the most important factor in your investment returns is that the type of assets you want to own in an inflation are exactly opposite from the type of assets you want to own in the deflation. So this is the first issue to be addressed.

Why Inflation?

My thesis is simple: The current financial leaders of the country much prefer inflation to deflation, and they have all the tools they need to get their way – at least for a while. They have shown by word and by deed they have every intention of avoiding deflation, which they confuse with a depression, and I see no reason to try to second-guess them. As a result, my purpose in this book is to persuade you that regardless of any short-term trends in recession-impacted prices, the US is headed down the inflationary path at an unprecedented speed, and there are specific, immediate steps you must take to survive and thrive in this new economy.

About 10 years after Alan Greenspan accelerated growth in the M2 money supply, new Fed Chairman Bernanke announced early in 2006 that the Fed would stop publishing the M3 money supply numbers. Without getting too technical, M1 is essentially printed currency, M2 adds bank deposits and other nearer forms of cash, and M3 is the broadest measure of money available in the economy. At the time they made this announcement they were trying to stimulate the economy, and while the M1 money supply was barely growing, M3 was growing at about 8% a year.

The Fed's excuse for stopping publishing M3 was that it wasn't of much use to anyone and that cost too much to collect the data. So after that announcement, one person with a personal computer started publishing the data at ShadowStats.com. Not surprisingly, M3 began to grow at faster and faster rates, culminating in about a 17% annual growth rate at the end of 2007. After that the Fed began their new policy of "quantitative easing" which simply means printing money. They did not acknowledge this new policy until almost a year later, but it was obvious in the numbers. The growth rate in M3 slowly retreated back below 8% while the growth rate in M1 shot up to 17%.

Why Print Money?

Printing money stimulates the financial markets, because that's where new money flows first until it can be redeployed into the real economy. When that happens, it stimulates the real economy. It also, importantly, lowers the value of the dollar.

Why would the Fed and the Treasury Department want to lower the value of the dollar? The first and most important reason is that it reduces the government's debt load in real terms. It is simply cheaper to pay back debt with inflated dollars than with dollars of stable value or even, in a deflation, increasing value. Specifically, inflation reduces the value of foreign debt holding. Essentially we spent many years giving the Chinese green paper in return for real physical goods. Now, by continually lowering the value of the dollar, we can erode the value of that green paper to a smaller amount or even zero.

In like manner, an inflated dollar lowers the consumer debt load in real terms. There's no easier way to see this than in the case of a house financed with a fixed-rate mortgage. An ever-inflating dollar drives up the value of the house while leaving the amount of the mortgage constant, making it very easy for the homeowner to repay the mortgage from the inflated dollars arriving via cost of living adjustments in his salary. (Actually, the value of the house is constant but the value of the dollar declines, so the price of a house in dollars has to rise to maintain parity with other goods and services.)

Lowering the value of the dollar also shrinks the real burden of various government unfunded liabilities, most notably Social Security. Although Social Security is supposed to be adjusted for the consumer price index, by manipulating the calculation of the CPI the government can keep the growth rate of Social Security benefits well below the level of inflation. And as you undoubtedly know, there is nothing in the Social Security Trust Fund except a bunch of IOUs from the government that can only be paid in two ways. One is by raising tax rates on the employed population, primarily young people. The other is by letting people's salaries rise at an inflated rate to keep pace with the dollar decline, thus generating enough revenue with current tax rates to cover the annual Social Security obligation. Technically, the government will have kept its promise to pay a certain amount of dollars to retirees. The fact that those dollars are not sufficient to buy food and shelter is hard cheese for the folks who were relying on it.

Dollar Down, Inflation Up – Get Used To It

My long-term thesis in this book is that the dollar will keep declining and high inflation will be the environment in which you have to invest. I also think it is *possible* that the Fed will lose control of this slippery slope they are pushing the dollar down and the US will go into hyperinflation. Regular inflation can be very unpleasant with double-digit rates of price increases. Hyperinflation involves triple-digit rates of price increases and is a catastrophe for those who are not prepared. It is difficult to manage a business or a family budget in a hyperinflationary environment. The policies of the last two administrations and the inclinations of the last two Fed Chairmen have put the United States at risk of a hyperinflationary outcome. It may not happen – I certainly hope it doesn't – but you need to be prepared for it. That is a measure of the risk to our country and economy from the foolish policies we now see being implemented every day. Sadly, many other countries in the rest of the world are in no better shape.

Those of us who predicted the credit crisis, weakening dollar, and the predictably dysfunctional response of the government now find ourselves split into two camps: the inflationists and the deflationists. The deflationists point to falling prices of housing, commercial real estate, automobiles, commodities and other assets as proof that deflation rules the day. They anticipate a virtually endless housing slowdown with falling prices as we get more Alt-A and Option ARM mortgage implosions. They believe consumers will be squeezed for years by poor credit ratings, employment pressures, and an attitudinal change towards saving from consuming. They point out that profit margins in the United States corporations are falling, there won't be any more Fed cuts because they are out of bullets, and all the geopolitical risks that affect oil are still in place.

The inflationists point to the rapid growth in the money supply and the dramatic leveraging of the Fed's balance sheet as proof that inflation will rule the future.

In the short term, I believe the Fed is done cutting interest rates (affecting the price of money). This may seem obvious since the Fed funds rate is now in a 0.00% to 0.25% range, and many commentators have said that the Fed can't cut below 0%. Why not? There's no reason the Fed could not begin paying banks to take federal funds, especially if the credit came with strings attached like it had to be re-lent into the economy instead of simply used to buy Treasury bonds. However, the Fed has signaled that they have switched to quantitative easing (affecting the amount of money), and I believe they will continue to print money and create credit until they perceive the crisis is over. In that environment, we should expect the dollar to be to resume its decline and commodities to resume their advances. I am an inflationist.

Inflation or Deflation?

The very first question about our collective financial future and how you should structure your investments is whether we are headed for inflation or deflation. Almost no one believes that Fed Chairman Bernanke can walk the knife blade between those two so skillfully that he can find a middle way out of the morass. Most of us believe the problems are now so large, thanks in part to the Fed's own actions over the last 15 years, that it isn't a

question of skill – no one can get us out of this without an inflation, a deflation, or both.

My position is that we are in for several years of double-digit
inflation, with a real possibility that it evolves into hyperinflation.
In fact, the thing I most abhor about the government's policies is
not the wastefulness of the bailouts and the obvious cronyism, but
that Bernanke has put the country's future at risk of hyperinflation.
We never should have even come close to this point.

If there is only double-digit inflation, it can eventually be
managed down to single-digit, and then back to the low single-digit
level that passes for stable monetary policy. "Mild" 2% inflation
reduces the value of a dollar by 25 cents in only 15 years. In 35
years the value of a dollar has been cut in half; this is less than the
working lifespan of most people, so "mild" inflation plays hell with
their retirement plans. After 70 years, only three generations, the
$1.00 is worth only 25 cents. And that outcome is the good news.

If Bernanke loses it and there is a hyperinflation, it will be
followed by a deflationary crash. That always happens.

Why The "Deflation First" Argument Is Wrong

There are certainly some major deflationary forces afoot in
our economy, and "Deflation or Inflation?" is the $64 (deflation)
or $64 million (inflation) question. In order to write this book on
the inflationary outcome, I sought out arguments for the opposite
case to think through their points. So I was glad to find a publication from Bob Prechter of *The Elliot Wave Theorist* titled "Market
Myths Exposed." His Myth #3 is "Worry About Inflation Instead
of Deflation."

Bob is one of the most articulate spokesmen for the opposite
point of view, and believes a deflationary crash will come first,

followed by a hyperinflation. I want to summarize his argument, which leads him to fight the Fed, and show you exactly where I think he is wrong.

Bob is a Yalie, but I don't hold that against him. Some of my best friends are Yalies. There is an old story about a Harvard guy and a Yale guy who walk into the men's room together and relieve themselves. The Yalie stops at the washbasin, but the Harvardian heads for the door. The Yalie says: "At Yale, we are taught to wash our hands before leaving the bathroom." The Harvard guy looks at him and says: "At Harvard, we are taught not to pee on our hands."

But I digress. Bob is a smart guy and has made some great market calls. However, his bias for years has been that there is going to be a Great Supercycle deflationary crash at some point. He made a Dow Jones forecast back around 1984, I think in *Barron's*, that caused me to write a letter to the editor pointing out that due to the way the DJIA is constructed, to hit Bob's forecast IBM would have to go to $5 a share. Even though we had lunch together after that, I think he had some bad feelings about my letter until I was caught in the tech stock crash. In 2002 he wrote *Conquer the Crash*, his most recent book on deflation, and even though the following five years were quite inflationary, he must feel pretty vindicated.

I look at Elliott Wave stuff, but most of the practitioners always seem to have an "alternative count" to explain why the theory is right, but their forecast was wrong. If you can get past that, Prechter is one of the most thoughtful of the group.

Prechter's Argument

The overview is that Prechter thinks we will have a deflationary crash, followed by a huge inflation as the Fed opens the money spigot. I think the Fed already has opened the money spigot, and we are going to have a huge inflation followed at some point in the future by a deflationary crash. So he and I simply differ on the order of things, but that is a difference that really makes a difference to what you do with your investments. Everything you want to own in an inflation – commodities, stocks, real estate, precious metals – will kill you in a deflation. And anything you want in a deflation – mainly cash and bonds – will leave you poor in an inflation.

Obviously, Prechter is aware of the bizarre level of government bailout spending, stimulus spending, rapid growth in the Fed's balance sheet, and size of the government's unfunded future liabilities like Social Security and Medicare.

But he argues that in spite of all the money printing, creditors (banks in particular) will stop lending. That will keep the credit supply from inflating. Debtors will default, as we are seeing in housing foreclosures, credit card default rates and bankruptcy filings. Now here's the key: He believes these forces will "overwhelm" the government and Fed efforts to inflate, resulting in deflation. So he is betting that the Fed does not have the tools and power they need to achieve the goal they want. He is betting against the Fed (and the European Central Bank).

As evidence, he points out that in the great inflations of history, the money supply exploded higher. Interest rates went to double and then triple digits. Commodity and stock prices shot up. Consumer prices shot up. People can't wait to get rid of their paper dollars.

Prechter then argues that today, none of those things are happening. M3, which is no longer calculated by the Fed but is available from ShadowStats.com, is falling at the fastest clip since the 1930s:

Annual U.S. Money Supply Growth - SGS Continuation
Monthly Average through Aug. 2010 (Source:St Louis Fed, SGS)

— M1   M2   M3 SGS

Published: Sep. 16, 2010   shadowstats.com

Interest rates on Treasury bills are stuck at zero. The Commodity Research Bureau index of commodity prices is half of what it was two years ago, and the stock market is lower than it was 10 years ago. Producer and consumer prices are not going up. People are hanging onto their dollars, banks are hanging onto their dollars, and Wal-Mart is cutting prices. In his view, the deflation has already begun.

But Wait...

In fact, total new credit in the U.S. has continued to increase because the Fed is buying Treasury bonds to monetize a $1.6 trillion annual government deficit. Private credit may be stalled or falling, but government credit is more than replacing it – just as the Keynesians running the economy believe should happen.

Before we get into Myth #3, I do not understand why Prechter thinks the Fed would allow a deflationary crash before they caused the huge inflation. Unless Bob believes for some reason that the Fed does not have the tools or wherewithal to prevent a deflationary crash, I just don't get it.

He has said: "The Fed and the Treasury have bailed out or guaranteed another trillion or two of bad debt and promise to do even more." In fact, the guarantees to Fannie Mae and Freddie Mac alone exceed $10 trillion, and it should be obvious that the Fed can guarantee commercial paper, bank holding company debt, corporate loans or anything else it wants to lend its AAA credit rating to. General Electric would be in bankruptcy today if the government didn't guarantee its debt, keeping its interest payments at less than half of what the free market would make them pay.

My view is entirely different. The three forces of deflation I have identified for you are the credit implosion due to the generational shift, the demographics of baby boomers getting to retirement age, and technology driving prices down at a never-before-seen rate. These are powerful forces. Arrayed against them are a Federal Reserve and Administration determined not to let those forces overwhelm the economy.

Which brings me back to Myth #3. First, Bob points out that banks now are 95% invested in debt backed by mortgages, whereas they used to be 40% in Treasury bonds. So if the value of mortgages declines by 80%, as he expects in a housing bust, most banks will be out of business.

But much of the "debt backed by mortgages" actually is bonds from Fannie Mae and Freddie Mac, and it is quite clear those are backed by the full faith and credit of the U.S.; they are a T-bond substitute. So the situation is not nearly as dire as appears on the surface.

The 80% decline in the value of mortgages is a circular argument: "I believe deflation is coming, so mortgages will fall in value 80%, so the banks will be bankrupt, and that is deflationary." Uh, yeah. But the fall in mortgage values can't cause deflation via bank failures if it requires an already-existing deflation to cause the fall in mortgage values in the first place. Also, the odds of Fannie Mae and Freddie Mac bonds falling 80% in a deflation, which is when bonds go up in value, are slim. That might happen if they were private enterprises and defaulted, but government-guaranteed debt doesn't default in nominal terms. The government "defaults" by *in*flating the dollar, so the bondholder gets back the promised 100 cents on the dollar, but the 100 cents is not worth nearly what it was when the bond was purchased.

Then, Bob argues that commercial mortgage loans are going bad, banks have been lending to consumers instead of businesses that actually generate income to pay back loans, most mortgage lending is by the government and not the banks, people are walking away from their homes and mortgages, and so on – all of which cause the banks to restrict lending, which is deflationary. True enough. What he does not point out is that the Fed has pumped in or guaranteed trillions in new credit, including funding the stimulus spending, specifically to offset this "problem." Not only that, but this is the second time the U.S. has kept short-term rates ridiculously low to let the banks borrow cheaply, buy higher-yielding Treasury bonds, and use the spread to safely rebuild their balance sheets. Former Fed Chairman Alan Greenspan pulled this off successfully in the early 1990s, and Ben Bernanke is showing he learned the lesson well.

After a few more points related to the collapse in bank lending, Bob mentions that the FDIC is out of money. This is not news, nor is it important. Once again, the government can simply appropriate money to go to the FDIC, and sell T-bonds or bills to fund it. If the Chinese or other buyers don't want the debt, the Fed can create money and buy the bonds. This is *in*flationary, not *de*flationary. In fact, any form of money or credit weakness is only an argument for *de*flation if you assume the Fed will do nothing about it. But as we've seen, the Fed is ready to back pretty much anything or any institution as needed, so all of these obvious weaknesses are actually an opportunity for more Fed money creation, and therefore more *in*flation.

Finally, Prechter argues that many states are broke and approaching insolvency, and this is deflationary. How? Does anyone really believe the Fed won't bail out the states, too? Is the political class going to tell California to slash pensions, going into an election? It's time to get real, folks. Citicorp's bondholders were bailed out, the Greek government is going to be bailed out, Goldman Sachs got 100 cents on the dollar for $19 billion in credit default swaps with AIG. California is going to be bailed out. I don't even think there is a legal mechanism for a state to file for bankruptcy.

The Money Supply

So what is going on with the money supply? As a quick reminder, M1 (the lighter gray line at the lowest level in 2007 on the last graphic) is currency and checking deposits. When the Fed "prints money" both real and in the form of credit, M1 goes up. You can see that the growth rate in M1 was in the 0% to 2% range for four years from early-2005 to mid-2008, when the Fed suddenly put the pedal to the metal and shot the growth rate up into the 16% to 18% range. That is banana republic-style money growth, and it was their panic reaction to the recession they didn't see coming.

Although the growth rate of M1 came down dramatically as the Fed decided the economy was past the point of maximum danger, it remains well above the levels where it was for most of the 'Noughties.

M2, the middle line in the 2007 era, simply adds savings accounts to M1. It's a bigger number than M1, so the Fed bump up has less impact. The decline seems to include both the Fed's curtailment of M1 and some people using up their savings.

M3 is M2 plus time deposits, like certificates of deposit (CDs). The saver can't get to this money quite so quickly. The numbers since 2005, when the Fed stopped calculating M3, come from John Williams at ShadowStats.com. He implies that people poured money into CDs and the like in 2006, 2007.and the first part of 2008. They then reversed their behavior on a dime and started cashing in their CDs as soon as possible.

Well, maybe. I sure don't remember 2006 and 2007 that way. But if people really did roughly double the growth rate of M3 during that period, and then began cashing everything in as soon as the economy hit the fan – so what? Assuming the numbers are even correct, why should an outsized increase not be corrected in the following period by an outsized decrease?

So while I know it is important to keep an eye on M1 and M2, I don't see anything there that screams "deflation" today. And I think the M3 numbers are pretty squishy ground to try to make the same case.

All the rest of Prechter's arguments are just a way of saying we have been through a tough recession, and it is early in the recovery. Of course interest rates on Treasury bills are stuck at zero. Bernanke is holding them there "for an extended period" until the recovery is on solid ground, not dependent on further government stimulus and quantitative easing.

Commodity prices are half of what they were two years ago because the price of oil is down from $147 to just over half that. Oil was below $35 in January 2009 – does the fact that it doubled in the following year fit with deflation or inflation? As the government stimulus hits the economy in the U.S., Europe and China, I expect the demand for all commodities to trend higher, not lower. The stock market, consumer and producer prices will all follow the economy up. They show where we have been, not where we are going.

Has the Inflation Already Begun?

Doctrinaire anything drives most of us crazy, but doctrinaire monetarists may take the cake. Right now, they are saying the inflation is here, because inflation is a measure of the increase in the money supply, not a measure of the increase in prices. So even though consumer and producer prices are low, and some commodities periodically fall in price, that all means nothing. The Fed has printed the money, so inflation is here.

My Dad once asked me: "How many legs does a lamb have?"

Of course I said: "Four."

Dad: "Right. And if we define the tail as a leg, now how many legs does the lamb have?"

I said: "Five."

Dad: "Wrong. The answer is four. Just because you call a tail a leg, doesn't make it a leg."

The monetarists define inflation as an increase in the money supply, and then smugly inform the rest of us that inflation is already raging, even if the prices of things aren't going up. After all, the Fed has created $1.5 trillion in new money and, partnered with the Treasury Department, has guaranteed or bailed out many trillions of toxic debt. Our Congress is spending money like the proverbial drunken sailor, and the Fed is monetizing the deficits.

Central banks around the world have been doing the same thing. How can this not end in a huge inflation?

Well, I think it will. But I will not try to tell you that runaway inflation is already here, when you just have to look around you to see it isn't true under the conventional definition of inflation as an increase in prices. It isn't just the *quantity* of money that counts, it is also the *velocity* of money that, multiplied together, equal nominal GDP. As long as velocity falls as fast as quantity rises, nominal GDP won't grow and there will be no inflation in prices. Right now, the banks are sitting on all the money the Fed has pumped into them, killing velocity.

Where the monetarists have it right is pointing out that once the money is created and in the system, it is *politically* very difficult to withdraw it. Unless there is robust economic activity going on, the effect of the Fed "taking away the punchbowl" will be to end the party before it begins. That exposes a lot of politicians to being voted out of office by angry citizens, so the Fed has to move very carefully. Yet once the money is created, if velocity starts accelerating then inflation will increase rapidly, and the Fed is certain to be well behind the 8-ball in (a) detecting it, and then (b) doing something about it that (c) eventually has an impact.

So inflation has *not* already begun, as Bob Prechter points out. But the danger of inflation beginning any minute is very, very high.

The Fed "Can't" Create Enough Credit (???)

The argument that the Fed can't create enough credit to save the economy is one of the most baffling positions the deflationists hold. Prechter argues that the banking system is broken, and banks have so many bad loans on their books that they are ruined. He says they can't borrow any new money because they are already underwater. Consumers are also broke, so they can't borrow more money, either. Therefore unlimited Fed credit is irrelevant, because no one can afford to pay banks interest anymore.

I live on a different planet. On my planet, if you create a Cash for Clunkers program, people will rush to buy cars. If the Fed buys toxic loans from the banks at 100 cents on the dollar, banks will make new loans. Maybe only 50 cents in new loans, but loan officers get paid to produce. If the Fed doesn't think the banks are making loans fast enough, guidelines will be created with lower FICO scores and interest coverage ratios, and the banks will be told to lend. If the government wants people to buy houses, they will loan money directly through the FHA at 3.5% down, with fixed rate mortgages under 5%. If that doesn't work, they will lower the interest rate to 4%...3%...2%...1%, and lower the required FICO score to boot. And the Fed will monetize all the FHA's debt, all day long.

Hyperinflation...when?

Prechter seems to agree there will be hyperinflation in the U.S., but only *after* the deflationary bust. He believes hyperinflation could only happen after a bond market implosion. We have to have a banking crisis, with thousands of banks going under, unemployment at 33%, the municipal bond market destroyed and a panic in government bonds. After this apocalypse, the politicians would take control of the printing press, and we could have hyperinflation. Prechter says either the government would take over printing money, and we would go back to Treasury notes from Federal Reserve notes, or they would force the Fed to monetize new federal debt.

My question is: If printing money and monetizing the Federal debt would get us out of a deflationary bust, why won't the Fed *prevent* the deflationary bust in the first place? Why does anyone need to "force" the Federal Reserve to monetize new federal debt, when they are gleefully doing it every day? Why would the Fed let "thousands" of banks go under, when they can simply merge bad banks out by guaranteeing the acquiring bank against all losses on a loan portfolio? Why let the municipal bond market be destroyed, when all the Fed has to do is guarantee all municipal bonds? Issuing that order would take less than an hour.

In short, why would the Fed allow a deflationary bust to start that would end its independence and cause virtually every politician to be thrown out of office, if as Prechter admits it has the tools to end a deflationary bust? And why, especially, would Ben Bernanke, a leading scholar about the Great Depression and avowed enemy of another depression, not use those tools to prevent it from happening? I just don't get it.

After looking at the evidence, I think the argument for deflation before inflation is simply betting against the Fed. Warren Buffet says Rule #1 of investing is "Don't lose money," and Rule #2 is "Don't forget Rule #1." I'd add that Rule #3 must be "Don't bet against the Fed," and Rule #4 is "Don't forget Rule #3." I bet against the Fed once; it was a very painful experience. The bottom line is that Prechter's Myth #3 runs into Murphy's Rule #3, and gets run over by it. Inflation is coming, big time.

The deflationary apocalypse has an emotional appeal to those who believe the bad financial behavior of the last 15 years deserves to be punished, but I believe Prechter has it bass-ackwards. The Fed will fight the real deflationary forces of credit contraction, demographics and technology tooth and nail. They will, accidentally or on purpose, cause an accelerating inflation that will be very difficult to contain. If they can "pull a Volker" and get it under control, they will probably be praised for saving the financial system, even though they were the root of the problem. If it gets away from them, we'll have a hyperinflation and *then* the bust. Either way, you should be preparing for accelerating and eventually high inflation, not Prechter's deflation. There will be a time to worry about the deflationary bust scenario. It is not now.

CHAPTER 2

The Bernanke Fed

He that won't be counseled can't be helped.
—Benjamin Franklin

n practice, the effectiveness of anti-deflation policy could be significantly enhanced by cooperation between the monetary and fiscal authorities. A broad-based tax cut, for example, accommodated by a program of open-market purchases to alleviate any tendency for interest rates to increase, would almost certainly be an effective stimulant to consumption and hence to prices. Even if households decided not to increase consumption but instead re-balanced their portfolios by using their extra cash to acquire real and financial assets, the resulting increase in asset values would lower the cost of capital and improve the balance sheet positions of potential borrowers. A money-financed tax cut is essentially equivalent to Milton Friedman's famous 'helicopter drop' of money." —*Ben S. Bernanke, November 21, 2002*

In spite of his notorious "helicopter" quote, I like Ben Bernanke as a person. He seems intelligent and certainly has spent a lot of time thinking about the Fed, what it should and shouldn't do, how it should and shouldn't act. He was born in Georgia and grew up in Dillon, South Carolina in one of the few Jewish families in that area. Like me, he went to public schools and then on to Harvard College for an AB in economics. He's a smart and accomplished guy, starting as editor of his high school newspaper, class valedictorian, All-State saxophonist, and booking the highest SAT scores in South Carolina the year he took them – 1590 out of 1600.

I graduated from Harvard *cum laude* and went into the business world, but he graduated *summa cum laude* went on to get a Ph.D. in economics from MIT. After teaching at Stanford and NYU he became a tenured professor at Princeton and then chairman of their economics department. He was a member of the Board of Governors of the Federal Reserve from 2002 to 2005, and got to watch Alan Greenspan handle the aftermath of the dotcom crash and create the U.S. real estate bubble. On February 1, 2006, he was appointed to a four-year term as Chairman of the Board of Governors of the Federal Reserve System. Normally, the chairmanship is renewed for the full 14 year term of a member of the Board.

In addition to being a former editor of the *American Economic Review*, he's been labeled one of the 50 best economists in the world. His specialty is the economic and political causes of the Great Depression. In a famous quote that brought down the house at Milton Friedman's 90th birthday party in 2002, he said: "Let me end my talk by abusing slightly my status as an official representative of the Federal Reserve System. I would like to say to Milton and Anna, regarding the Great Depression: You're right, we did it. We're very sorry. But thanks to you, we won't do it again."

Later that same year, in a speech to the National Economists Club titled "Deflation: Making Sure 'It' Doesn't Happen Here," he presented the "helicopter" quote at the beginning of this introduction, and ever after has been nicknamed "Helicopter Ben."

Note that he was quoting Milton Friedman, whom no one ever called "Helicopter Milton." But this bit of unfairness is only the beginning of Ben Bernanke's problems. (Note: The whole 2002 speech is in Appendix A of this book, and is well worth reading as a roadmap to the Bear Stearns bailout, the destruction of the U.S. dollar and, of course, the scrambling of the helicopters that is already underway.)

In this speech on deflation, Bernanke was simply making an obvious point. In a fiat or paper money system, the central bank owns the printing presses that are the physical means of creating money. Since they control the printing presses, they can always avoid deflation by simply issuing more money. One can argue what "money" really means, or whether or not the government is printing enough of it to have an impact, but there's no denying the underlying principle. Yet it seemed to gall many people that someone would say out loud out what everyone knew to be true but didn't want to talk about.

Nice Guy, Wrong Job

To paraphrase the old saying about greatness, some men are born mediocre, some achieve mediocrity and some have mediocrity thrust upon them. Ben Bernanke certainly was not born mediocre and he has a record of outstanding achievement. But he is dedicated to defending the fiat money system and avoiding economic weakness during a time when our country faces those three unprecedented deflationary challenges:

1. The worst credit-based deflation since the Great Depression, including a dramatic adjustment in housing prices back down to their long-term trend level, driven by a new generation that hates debt

2. The demographic impact of the retirement of the baby boomer generation

3. The now-meaningful impact of the New Economy that evolved from the dotcom revolution

Due in large part to the Fed's response to these challenges, the dollar is losing strength as the world's reserve currency, and a huge legacy of debt in unfunded government mandates almost requires a period of economic weakness to force a non-inflationary resolution of these serious problems. The situation calls for a "willow tree" response to bend with the inevitable changes, yet be strong enough to survive the storm. Instead, we are getting the "King Canute" response, as the entire Bernanke Fed tries to hold back the tide. Or perhaps the "oak tree" response, where the tree tries harder and harder not to bend until it is catastrophically uprooted and destroyed.

The solutions Bernanke is comfortable with – the ones he has advocated during his entire academic career – simply are not the ones that can effectively deal with our underlying problems. It would take an intellectual transplant for him to advocate the "tough love" policies that, sooner or later, will have to be implemented to deal with these challenges and shape a positive future for America. The right path is out there for both our country (Part IV, below) and our individual investments (Chapter 12), but the Bernanke Fed is committed to a different, dead-end road.

Bernanke was criticized early in his term as Fed Chairman for moving too slowly to deal with the expanding impacts of the subprime mortgage crisis. In this case "moving too slowly" essentially meant exposing Wall Street and the banks to suffering the consequences of the bubble they built on the backs of unqualified borrowers. For a while I hoped perhaps this was his way of signaling a dramatic change in policy, but as it turned out he *was* moving too slowly given that he had already accepted the Wall Street/banking agenda. Once he started cutting interest rates rapidly in January 2008 and creating new forms of lines of Fed credit, the reputation rehabilitation process began on the op-ed pages, praising what a good job he was doing. At this point, he has been completely co-opted by the establishment and almost certainly will have "mediocrity thrust upon him."

When Bernanke was appointed Chairman, I predicted in print in my *New World Investor* newsletter than he would not finish his term. I stand by that, and am expanding it to say that all these good people on the Fed will, collectively, treat the symptoms of problems in our economy and fail to respond to the underlying problems. Their medicine will create new, worse problems, and that is why I've labeled this "the worst Fed regime ever." They really "won't do it again." They'll do something different, and much worse.

The dramatic demographics of baby boomers retiring, the housing and credit deflations feeding into the Gen X and Millennial generation ascendency, and the impact of the New Economy will create intense deflationary pressures for many years. Because these pressures come at a time of very high levels of debt on both consumer and government balance sheets, Ben Bernanke is going to be fighting a war during his entire term as Chairman that will make Vietnam or Iraq look like a walk in the park. He will use the tools that worked in the last few financial battles, but will not work in the new realities. The side effects of this Fed's policies – an ever-weakening dollar, accelerating inflation and a yo-yo tax policy – will have a major impact on your personal financial situation, whether you are 25, 45, or 65; rich, middle-class or poor; a stockholder, bondholder, or up to your neck in credit card debt.

Ben Bernanke is the wrong man in the wrong place at the wrong time. He is not going to save you. You're going to have to do it yourself. I wrote this book primarily to help you not only survive but prosper during the worst Fed regime ever.

I also have a faint hope that somehow, somewhere, a politician will read Part IV of this book and demand our country get on a path to solve our problems instead of papering them over with green paper. It could happen, but that's not the way to bet.

The Bernanke Box

Although the Chairman says he is about to start tightening up, I don't believe him. It must have been four years ago that I first used the term: "The Bernanke Box." The box is that the level of credit creation and money printing required to keep the economy growing is much larger than the level of credit creation and money printing that will set off a major inflation and kill the dollar. The only thing that has changed in four years is that the Bernanke Box has assumed a coffin-like shape.

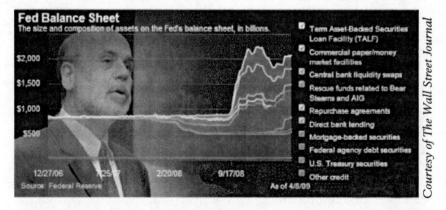

This graphic shows the incredible expansion in the Fed's balance sheet as they added toxic mortgage assets from the banks at the end of the Bush administration. Assets more than doubled from under $1 trillion to well over $2 trillion. Almost all the growth was in "Short-term lending to Financial Firms and Markets" as then-Treasury Secretary Hank Paulson bailed out his Wall Street buddies. But while this has been running down, as shown by the much-reduced numbers above the "Traditional Portfolio and Long-Term Assets" line, Chairman Bernanke has replaced it with a rapid growth in long-term assets.

The St. Louis Fed believes this dramatic growth will continue. The Fed will continue buying mortgages and related securities, although at a slower rate. In addition, they have lent, spent or – most dangerous – guaranteed over $12.5 trillion in debt. That includes the whole mortgage finance system in the U.S., including Fannie Mae and Freddie Mac, which has at this point about $1 trillion in unrealized losses. In 2009, Fannie and Freddie made 87% of all housing loans. The FHA piled on with many loans made with 3.5% down payments. The government is making a huge bet that they can keep housing prices from collapsing further.

And they also can make that bet pay off, simply by allowing inflation to bring the price of housing and incomes up, while the debt payments stay level. That way, the only losers are the debt holders who put up the money for all these fixed interest mortgages: The taxpayers and buyers of Treasury bonds.

The Fed's assets form the base of our monetary system. The more assets grow, the more money and credit become available to the banking system. The faster the money supply grows, the more likely inflation will take off and the faster the value of the dollar will fall, maybe not against all currencies, but certainly against all commodities. Since the Fed began their reckless bet, the value of the dollar against a trade-weighted basket of currencies has fallen 15%. Doubling of the monetary base will double prices in five to seven years, which equals an inflation rate of 10% to 15%. Double-digit inflation is coming, and Bernanke can't stop it without causing an economic depression that would cost him his reputation and his job. So he won't stop it.

Inflation at those rates would have two effects. First, the biggest bubble in the history of the world, the 28-year bull market in U.S. Treasury bonds, would explode. Not just pop, explode. The Treasury bond market is huge, and both U.S. pension funds and foreign currency reserves are heavily invested in 20- and 30-year Treasuries. The geopolitical impact of the destruction in bond market wealth will be large and unpredictable. But I think the Fed will risk it, rather than the certain impact of a deep depression on their highly-leveraged balance sheet. No one talks about it, but the only way to pay back our national borrowing to cover decades of deficits is to make the dollar worth much, much less.

Today, our national debt is about $13.5 trillion, and there are about 100 million households, so the average American family owes $135,000. That's more than most people owe on their mortgage. At today's 3.3% interest rate, the U.S. spends about $445 billion a year on interest. The government takes in about $1 trillion a year in income taxes, and 44.5% of it goes for interest. They also take in another $1 trillion in corporate and other taxes. Much of the debt is short-term. If our creditors start worrying about inflation, what will they demand for an interest rate to roll it over? Will the Fed step in and buy the debt at low rates by printing more money, which will make our creditors even more worried about inflation and even less likely to buy new debt? And assuming President Obama is re-elected, by the time he leaves office the debt is forecasted to be well over $20 trillion. Our annual interest expense is going to go up substantially. But only about 50 million people in the country pay any meaningful income taxes – how much more can be loaded on the middle class before they buckle, or on "the rich" before they cut and run?

The second effect would be a flight to safety in stocks, real estate, hard assets and soft commodities. The high inflation rates of the 1970s made life miserable for stocks, because high interest rates bring down the price/earnings ratio people will pay for stocks. But in a full-fledged inflationary panic, the ability to raise prices and earnings will help stocks this time around (see the next chapter), plus they will be a haven for all the money coming out of the bond market. In the U.S., the people who own most of the bonds understand value and defensive stocks. The foreigners who own large amounts of bonds (China, Japan, Brazil) understand hard assets and commodities. Once fear becomes widespread that the value of the dollar will continue to fall, perhaps to the point it is no longer the world's reserve currency, there will be a self-fulfilling prophecy positive effect on stocks, real estate and commodities.

At some point in the next few years, some of our creditors are going to stop believing in our ability to pay our debts in uninflated money. We can't go on forever spending money we don't have to prop up our entitlement culture and create new entitlements, while printing money to prop up our banks and mortgage market. But with the current political system, the best government money can buy, there is almost no one with the courage and strength to change things before a crisis hits. The only one who can protect you from the inevitable is you.

As one example of how the Fed makes decisions that are not in your long-term interest, during the Greek debt crises the Fed made a large currency swap line available to the European Central Bank. In addition, about 20% of the International Monetary Fund loan to backstop Greece's economy came from the U.S. Why?

The European banks that hold huge amounts of Greek, Spanish and Portugese debt add up to almost half of the primary dealer network for U.S. Treasury debt. (See chart next page.)

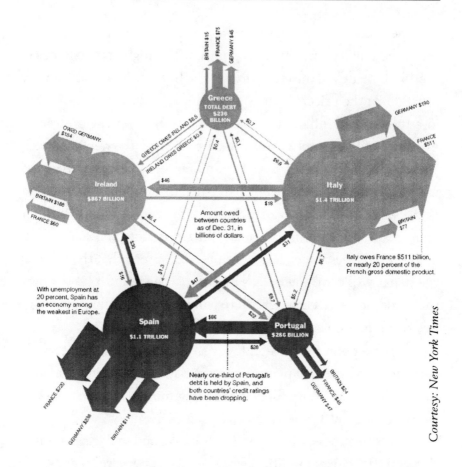

Courtesy: New York Times

If they failed, the primary Treasury dealer network would be cut in half overnight. The Treasury has to sell more debt in a month these days than it used to sell in an entire year. Maybe now we know why the U. S. taxpayer will be paying the very comfortable pension of a Greek government worker who retired at 53, and pays no taxes on their side business.

PART II
The Deflationary Forces

We must, indeed, all hang together or, most assuredly, we shall all hang separately.
—Benjamin Franklin

CHAPTER 3

The First Force: Demographics

THE AGING OF THE BABY BOOMERS

When the people find that they can vote themselves money,
that will herald the end of the republic.

—Benjamin Franklin

Threst of the three major deflationary forces facing the US economy is demographics. The baby boomer generation has had a dramatic impact on our economy from the time they started being born in 1946, but perhaps the most dramatic impact lies ahead as they retire.

The importance of demographics to the economy is that as we age we go through predictable spending patterns at different ages. After completing high school education at the age of 18, some enter the workforce and some go to college. Either way, by the age of 22 almost everyone is in the workforce and between the ages of 22 to 30 many people get married. Soon after that they have children and typically between the ages of 31 and 42 a family purchases their first house. Of course, that's the biggest investment that most families will make during their entire lives, and the most debt they will ever burden themselves with. But their spending continues to increase up to age 50 as they upgrade to a newer house, more furnishings, more cars and so forth. By about age 50 the youngest children reach their late teenage years or are starting to leave the household. From ages 50 to 60, family income remains high but spending starts to fall. The peak rate of investment is age 54. Families save more for retirement and pay down debt. Spending patterns change dramatically; for example, from buying furniture to leisure travel, which also peaks at age 54. Investment continues until about the age of 63 on average and net worth peaks between 64 and 65. After that, healthcare spending increases until the age of death, currently between 78 and 80.

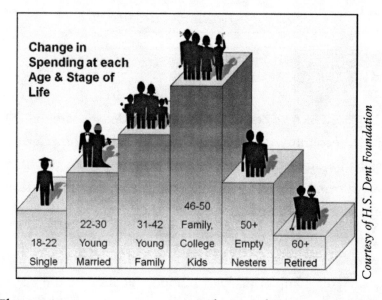

The impact on our economy is obvious, because consumers account for about 70% of our gross domestic product. The baby boomers have had a dramatic effect on the economy through the entire aging process, and are sometimes referred to as "the pig in the python." After World War II and into the 1950s, much of the spending was aimed at taking care of children. There was a large expansion of the public school system and family-oriented entertainment, such as amusement parks. In the 1960s, as the baby boomers entered college, the "cultural revolution" surprised many observers. The women's rights movement in the 1970s led to later marriages and a "baby bust" that saw many of the public school buildings built 20 years earlier closing for lack of students. First-home buying for the baby boomers began in earnest in the 1980s and continued into the 1990s. The oldest boomers, born in 1946, reached their peak spending year in 1994. The year with the largest number of births was 1957, and those folks reached their peak spending year in 2005.

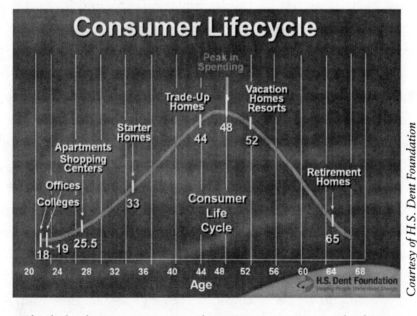

The baby boomers are now beginning to retire, which means much less spending overall and often downsized or relocated housing. Between now and 2023, when the boomers born in 1957

will reach 66, there will be an increasing deflationary force that our economy and government policy has not had to deal with before.

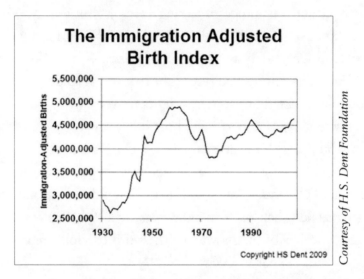

As you can see from the Immigration-Adjusted Birth Index chart, the long increase in births that includes the baby boomers actually started from a trough that ran from 1933 through 1936, in the depths of the Great Depression. Births peaked in 1957 and formed a long top that ran through 1964. The baby bust that followed 1964 ended in a trough that ran from 1973 through 1976. Another increase in births, the "Echo Baby Boom" began in 1977, as the oldest boomers turned 31, and ran up to a peak in 1990 at 4.16 million. The number of births then backed off a little to a trough of 3.88 million in 1997, a period I have labeled the "Echo Baby Bust." Steady growth since then saw the number of births in 2007 finally exceed the baby boomer peak in 1957 – 50 years later.

Most demographers think in terms of social generations – the Greatest Generation that fought World War II, or the Baby Boomers that have dominated postwar America. The number of people born in each social generation are:

Born During	Nickname	Number	Years Turning 48
1914-1924	Greatest Generation	32,303,000	1962-1972
1925-1945	Silent Generation	55,332,000	1973-1993
1946-1964	Baby Boomers	75,863,048	1994-2012
1965-1976	Generation X	41,144,037	2013-2024
1977-1994	Generation Y (Millennials)	67,948,526	2025-2042
1995- 2009+	Generation Z	61,365,000+	2043-2057+

Note: 2008 births estimated at 4,365,000 and 2009 births estimated at 4,400,000

But I prefer to look at economic generations, and a generation's impact on the economy depends on two things: (1) Are there more or less people every year hitting a particular age, and (2) what are their attitudes towards spending, saving, innovation and safety. Thus, it is not surprising that so many of the elementary schools that were built to overcome double session in the 1950s were being closed in the late 1970s and early 1980s. Overall, economic booms are associated with an increase of the number of people in their mid-40s, as we had from about 1986 to about 2002. Economic downturns are associated with a decline in that age group, which we are now facing. So here is the table above recast for economic generations instead of social generations, with the "Year Turning 48" now measured from the peak or trough year for births to capture the highest rate of change:

Born During	Nickname	Number	Year Turning 48	Economy
1909-1924	Greatest Generation	46,316,000	1969	Peaked
1925-1936	Depression Generation	30,805,000	1981	Bottomed one year later
1937-1964	Recovery Generation	100,390,048	2005	Peaked one year later
1965-1976	Baby Bust	44,144,037	2021	Should bottom 2021 or 2022
1977-1990	Echo Baby Boom	51,819,598	2038	Should peak 2038 or 2039
1991-1997	Echo Baby Bust	27,800,905	2045	Flattish through 2045
1998- 2009+	Next Generation	49,693,790+	**2055+**	Strong growth resumes

It may seem remarkable that one simple statistic can tell us that times probably will be tough through 2021, and then we will have another period of good economic growth for about 17 years to 2038 or 2039. After that, instead of a sharp decline our country is likely to see a flattish, stagnant economy for seven or eight years. Around 2045 or 2046, strong economic growth resumes for 10 years or more, depending on birth trends during the weak economic period we are entering.

Much of the work on popularizing the effects of demographics on the economy has been done by Harry Dent. Harry used to live in the next town up the coast from me in California, and we met once at my office to talk about the linkage between demographics and the stock market. He has been much taken to task by commentators because he predicted the Dow would go to 40,000 in one of his books during the boom. He later lowered that target to 32,000, and then lowered it again to something under 20,000. As he says himself, he got the direction right but the magnitude wrong.

To me, the effects of demographics on the economy are quite clear. I am not surprised that the link between demographics and the stock market is not nearly so clear, simply because there are numerous other factors that influence the level of the market besides consumer spending. Some commentators have made the mistake of thinking demographics are not particularly important simply because of Harry's prediction that the Dow would get to 40,000 before it broke in the great bull market. I think that's very wrong.

Throughout the history of the United States, we have tended to have booms that last 26 to 28 years followed by declines that last 12 to 14 years. There was a boom from 1902 to 1929, right through World War I, and then of course the Great Depression from 1930 until about 1942. After that, as World War II started to go us our way, we saw another boom from 1942 all the way to 1968. I joined American Express Investment Management in 1968, and I have clear memories of the last decline that lasted through 1982. In fact, I started the *California Technology Stock Letter,* my first investment newsletter, in January 1982. By the August 1982 bottom I was beginning to wonder if I was the only one who could see the values in technology stocks. I remember putting out an issue in that month that essentially said: "I have no idea why these stocks are so cheap, but I do know you need to absolutely load up on them." (See chart on next page)

Fortunately, the greatest boom began and it ran from 1983 through numerous recessions and crises in wars for 24 years to

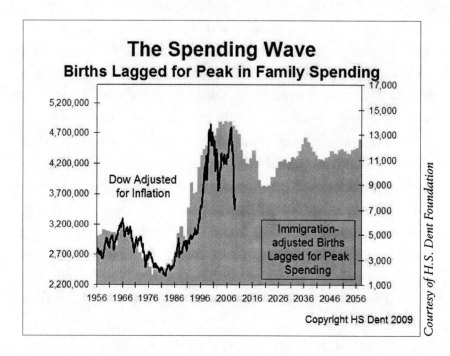

The Spending Wave
Births Lagged for Peak in Family Spending

Dow Adjusted for Inflation

Immigration-adjusted Births Lagged for Peak Spending

1956 1966 1976 1986 1996 2006 2016 2026 2036 2046 2056

Copyright HS Dent 2009

Courtesy of H.S. Dent Foundation

2006. In addition to the rising spending of the baby boomers, they have rising productivity as they get older and more experienced in their profession. That tends to drive costs down and keep inflation under control, even though demand is going up. Now, of course, we face a 12 to 14 year downturn driven by the downturn in births, with less total spending and productivity even though the per-person numbers probably will be little changed from the boomer generation.

Looking at the situation from the demographic point of view, it's clear that the stimulus programs and toxic asset buyouts that are the cornerstone of the Obama Administration's recovery plan simply do not address the underlying demographic forces. In the last boom, even through two Iraq wars, periodic stock market collapses in the 1987 Crash, the 1997 Asian currency collapse and the dotcom crash, natural disasters like Hurricane Katrina and soaring oil prices, the American consumer found ways to keep spending. People do not base their spending decisions on problems and disasters, they base them on their age and stage of life. That is what determines spending patterns. As they move through life, what they buy at each stage is consistent and predictable. How they change their spending, saving and investment patterns is very predictable. We went through a long period when the largest age cohort in the economy was earning and spending more each year. We are now going to go through a couple of decades where that same largest group is spending less, saving more and slowing the economy's growth. The echo baby boom generation will start a new expansion in 2023 that will last until about 2050.

But instead of constructing programs that addresses the declining population of heavy spenders, which would require the precision of a surgeon's scalpel, the administration is using policies more akin to a blacksmith's hammer. Chairman Bernanke and the Fed are determined to avoid a deflationary depression like the Great Depression of the 1930s, but they will have to print far more money and create far more credit than they are expecting to do in order to overcome the powerful deflationary drag of demographics. I have no doubt that they will make every effort to offset demographics with money and credit, but they aren't going to convince many retirees to buy a new ski boat. And there just aren't enough baby busters to buy ski boats, no matter how attractive the financing.

So Harry Dent and so many others would be right in forecasting a deflationary depression IF the Fed did not exist. But they do. They can create any amount of money and credit with the stroke of a pen, pushing up the prices of everything. That is inflation, not deflation. Selected assets like real estate may not keep up with the Great Inflation or hyperinflation coming, which is to say their prices could go down in real, inflation-adjusted terms.

But in nominal, current dollars, their prices will skyrocket. As we will see, stocks are an asset, and in every previous hyperinflation they have skyrocketed. So has gold and every other industrial or consumer product.

A Note On The Commodity Cycle

There does seem to be a roughly 30 year cycle in commodity prices during the last couple of hundred years, composed of about 20 to 23 years of flat prices and then five to 10 years of a rapid increase. The Commodity Research Bureau's broadest index only goes back to 1947, but the Producer Price Index is a good proxy for commodity cycles before that.

The PPI-adjusted CRB Index peaked in 1920 around 135, and even during the Roaring '20s boom, it fell back to 75. The Great Depression then took it down to 50, and it took World War II to launch the next upswing in 1942, 22 years after the prior peak.

The end of the war set off a sharp run up to touch 150 in 1949, with a correction back to 100 in 1950 and then a sharp upturn to the double top in 1951 just over 150. That was 31 years from the prior, 1920 top.

The CRB Index then retreated to 100 for a full 20 years, from 1952 to 1973. The guns-and-butter fiscal policies of the Vietnam War years set off the next CRB run, which topped at 300 in 1981, 30 years from the 1951 top. The Index fluctuated between 200 and 300 for the next 21 years, through 2002. It then took off again as the Fed slashed interest rates, and ran up to a peak of 460 in the fall of 2008, with $147 per barrel oil. That peak was 31 years from the prior peak.

The drop in commodity prices since then is reasonably interpreted by cycle theorists as the beginning of another 20 years of consolidation in commodity prices, perhaps between 250 and 350. But, thanks to Chairman Bernanke, that interpretation is going to be wrong. He is well aware that The Great Depression was *not* accompanied by a bust in commodity prices. That bust had happened 10 years before, in 1920. But this time, perhaps by chance, the commodity cycle coincides with the demographics cycle, making the deflationary pressures even more intense.

What to do? Inflate harder. Not only do commodity prices respond directly to inflation, as we saw in the Vietnam War years, but inflation gives the less-developed countries an opportunity to lift more of their citizens out of poverty. That 20% pay raise in China may barely keep up with 18% inflation, but the person who got it is more likely to support the government that made it possible. So the real demand for commodities will increase due to the Fed's monetary policies, as well as the nominal prices. I think the 30-year commodity price cycle is about to be hijacked by the Fed's printing press.

A Note on Real Estate

Spending on real estate is very predictable from demographic data. After coming out of college, people are looking for a job and an apartment. Office buildings and apartment buildings are the investments to be in to serve those aged 21 to 31. Shopping centers do well starting at age 26, as the new workers start building discretionary income. As people age, spending on starter homes happens, on average, at age 31. By age 42, trade-up homes are the place to be: More square footage, better finishes, better locations. The first peak for vacation home buying comes at age 48.

By that time, the average person has spent the bulk of what they will spend in their entire life on real estate. The first baby boomers hit age 48 in 1994, and the last will hit it in 2012. The biggest year for births was 1957, and they hit 48 in 2005 – virtually the peak for the real estate market.

There is a flurry of resort timeshare or home buying at age 55, and age 63 brings the second peak for vacation home buying, this time for permanent occupancy in retirement.

Home prices were essentially flat from 1940 through 2000 when adjusted for quality, size, inflation and interest rates. It was Alan Greenspan's fear of a Y2K meltdown that led him to slash interest rates before 2000, then quickly raise them to prevent inflation, which precipitated the dotcom crash. Then he slashed rates to near 1% and real estate prices adjusted for inflation and interest rates shot up 80% or more in only five years. Of course, we are now crashing back to 2000 levels, or maybe a little lower as the pendulum swings too far in the opposite direction.

The Fed and the Treasury are very worried about the real estate crash, which they should let play out. Lower house prices make it easier for Generation Y, born between 1977 and 1997, to buy their starter homes. Instead, the Fed is determined to flood even more money and stimulus into the housing sector to prevent the normal cycle from playing out. They will succeed for a while. Modified loans can be modified again if the borrower slips back into delinquency, and the now Government-owned Fannie Mae and Freddie Mac can keep raising their loan limits and lowering their credit standards until the housing market recovers. But it will take a lot more money to bail out real estate now than it would have in 1999, when the boomers were still buying trade-up houses. The cycle requires a 45% to 50% decline in home prices from the top to get back to the trendline. Bernanke & Co. may have moved too slowly to prevent that, as prices in many overbuilt areas already have declined that much.

CHAPTER 4

The Second Force: Generational Economics
THE RISE OF GENERATION X & THE MILLENNIALS

When the well's dry, we know the worth of water.
—Benjamin Franklin

T he second great deflationary force that the government must deal with is the 80-year cycle of changing generations. This is not the same as the demographics of the baby boom, although the boomers' sheer numbers increased their impact during their part of the 80-year cycle. This cycle is independent of the number of people in each cohort.

A generational cohort is defined as a group of individuals born around the same time who experience the same major economic and social events at roughly the same time of their lives. For example, the Depression Generation grew up during a period of scarcity, want, and economic instability. They typically were cautious about finances, thrifty and protective of their capital. The idea of generational cohorts was introduced by the sociologist Karl

Mannheim in the early 1920s, and then popularized by William Strauss and Neil Howe in their books, including *Generations* and *The Fourth Turning*.

Ideally, an 80-year cycle is comprised of four 20-year generational cohorts that experience the world in a predictable way. They each have a motivation, a function and a course of life that differs from the cohorts right before and right after them, but then are echoed in the next 80-year cycle by the cohort in the same relative position. Eighty years is a rough average, though, and the four cohorts are approximately 20 years each, but not exactly. In *The Fourth Turning*, Strauss and Howe classified every 20-year cohort and 80-year cycle since the War of the Roses cohort born from 1459 through 1487.

Eighty years has been the length of a typical long life. That may change dramatically in the near future, thanks to biotechnology and alternative health research. Many people don't realize that the first person to live to 150 is alive today, probably between 50 and 55 years old, with a 60% chance they are female. Still, unless there is productive research to extend the female reproductive cycle, the 20-year cohorts should remain unchanged. There just may be more of them alive at any one time in the future. We shall see.

Strauss and Howe called the first 20 years of the 80-year cycle the High Period. It is characterized by confident expansion as a "new normal" becomes established, following the collapse of the "old normal." This is a period of strong economic growth and awakening inflation.

The next 20 years they called the Awakening Period, characterized by a push back or rebellion against the new normal, and a search for new spiritual truths. This is a period of economic consolidation, but still with some growth, and stubbornly high inflation.

The third 20-year cohort is the Unraveling Period, when individualism increases and institutions established in the High Period begin to come apart. It is a troubled time full of cross-currents. Some sectors of the economy show remarkable growth, others stagnate, and there is a tendency to cut corners or use debt to try to keep economic growth going at the national level, or get rich at the individual level. Overall inflation often is quiescent during this period.

Finally comes the Crisis Period, which we entered in 2001, a time of crisis and upheaval as society gropes to understand or change its purpose and nature. This is a period of economic decline, often abrupt or dramatic, that is difficult to get out of. Deflationary forces seem to come out of nowhere, and investments made in the Unraveling Period under mild inflation assumptions suddenly go sour. Keeping up with the Joneses is so last generation and frugality is the new cool. Living within your means is not only necessary, it's sensible, even chic, and makes people feel smarter than the way they were living before (or than their parents lived). Our current Crisis Period won't end until around 2021.

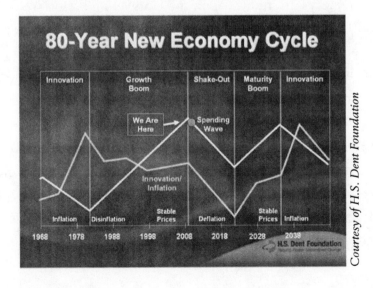

Courtesy of H.S. Dent Foundation

Dent points out that the classic 60 year Kondratieff cycle was two 30-year commodity cycles, one of rising prices and one of falling prices, that controlled commodity-based economies for centuries. But the importance of commodities to an agricultural or even 19th century industrial economy like Great Britain was replaced by the importance of the consumer, beginning around the Great Depression with mass production and the rise of the middle class. The Kondratieff cycle has been stretched to two 40-year cycles that make up an 80-year generational economic cycle.

Most recently, the Baby Boomers were born and grew up during a new 80-year cycle High Period. The old normal of Depression and war, committed marriages and low mobility in work and residence was replaced by expansion, rock 'n' roll, freer sex and more divorce, multiple careers and wandering. Then the Generation X Awakening Period pushed back hard against what was seen as self-centered Boomers.

The Millennial or Generation Y cohort was born and grew up as society suffered through the Unraveling Period from 1982 to 2001. It may seem odd to say "suffered" during that long bull market, but it isn't easy when old institutions are crumbling and being taken over by leveraged buyout artists. Stress levels are high as change accelerates, and it easy for people to misstep and see little or no progress in their real income or lives.

The New Silent Generation, a placeholder name invented by Strauss and Howe, runs from 2001 to about 2020, and includes my two youngest daughters. They will live surrounded by crisis and upheaval, and probably be less adventurous and risk taking than my two older Generation X kids.

Prophets – Born 1943-1960

Strauss and Howe called the first 20-year cohort of the 80-year cycle the Prophet Archetype. They grow up during the High Period, and are indulged, even spoiled, as children. It may be that the Prophets often have a higher number of births because their parents are living in optimistic, expanding times. They graduate from school into an Awakening Period, when they become crusaders for change. They are visionaries, inventors and innovators, and very entrepreneurial. They introduce dramatic changes in technologies and products, and even the way business is done.

They also are very moralistic, believing they know the right way, focused on themselves, willing to fight for what they believe in. They are driven by their values, which often differ dramatically from their parents. The 80-year cycle enters the Unraveling Period when they are 40 to 60 years old, and they provide moralistic leadership during these confusing times. During the following 20 year, the Crisis Period, they are the elder leaders providing a context to bridge over to the next High Period.

Nomads – Born 1961-1981

The second 20-year cohort is the Nomads Archetype. Their parents were busy changing the world during the Awakening Period, and had less time for them. So they grew up underprotected, perhaps even unwanted, and can be tough and cynical. They also are more diverse, as they had to make their own way from an early age, and adventurous because they know they can rely on themselves – they always have.

During this period, the economy is booming as the innovations of their parents move into the mainstream. They leave school into the semi-chaos of an Unraveling Period, which increases their alienation. But as they get to midlife, the Crisis Period confirms what they suspected: There was something really wrong for the last 40 years, and it wasn't them. Their coping skills and cynical attitudes make them street-smart leaders for the Crisis Period, and as they age they become tough-minded elders as the next High Period gets underway.

Heroes – Born 1982-2000

The third 20-year cohort is the Hero Archetype. This was the Greatest Generation, and will be echoed in the Millennial Generation. They grow up as increasingly protected children during the Unraveling Period. Their parents turn away from focusing on big social and economic causes, as is typical during the Awakening Period. They look inward to family, friends and the local community, where it seems possible to do something about the Unraveling. The Hero Archetype grows up in a close-knit family, and develops a trust in authority and institutions. They are conventional citizens, and perhaps because of that, feel very powerful.

This, even though the economy usually transitions during their childhood from reaping the last benefits of the prior innovation phase (new technologies, higher productivity) to flatter real growth and higher volatility. Instead of recessions, the economy is hit by a series of setbacks like the Asian debt crises and the various oil shocks that expose the most leveraged or vulnerable companies and sectors. New money is still made (think Google) but old models are simultaneously being destroyed (think GM).

The rising tide that lifted all the boats during the second 20-year cohort pauses at full flood.

The Heroes graduate from school into a Crisis Period, and they are ready to handle it with their teammates, under the direction of the authorities. As they hit midlife, the 80-year cycle turns to the High Period, and they feel rewarded for handling the Crisis Period and ready to ride the High. But in the next Awakening, they alternate between being considered the Heroes – a great generation – and being attacked as the gray flannel, button-down conformists that are blocking progress.

Artists – Born 1925-1942 and 2001-2021(?)

The fourth and final 20-year cohort of the 80-year cycle are the Artist Archetype. They grow up during a Crisis Period, as the tide goes from full flood to full ebb, and their parents over-protect them from the chaos around them. They can be emotional and indecisive, feeling inner conflict about what they would like to do versus the dangers around them. They also can be repressed by circumstances and parental caution and worry, and be very ready to compromise just to get along.

During this period the economy goes into a depression or deflationary bust. Companies that built overcapacity during the boom years, or failed to get to #1 or #2 in market share are in danger of bankruptcy, even if their business model is still working for those who did get most of the market share. It is a tough time for equity investors, and even bond investors must tread carefully due to dramatically increased credit risks.

The Artists graduate from school as the depression ends, into a High Period as sensitive young adults still not sure if the changes they are seeing are more chaos and crisis, or a good new thing. By midlife they are indecisive leaders during an Awakening Period, and by the time of the next Unraveling Period they are the empathetic elders, sensing a new Crisis Period coming.

During each of the 20-year cycles, society is made up of a different arrangement of these generational archetypes:

	Children	Young Adults	Midlifers	Elders
High Period	Prophets	Artists	Heroes	Nomads
Awakening Period	Nomads	Prophets	Artists	Heroes
Unraveling Period	Heroes	Nomads	Prophets	Artists
Crisis Period	Artists	Heroes	Nomads	Prophets

History shapes each generation, depending on which phase of life it is in during key historical events. A World War leaves a different impression on children than it leaves on the midlife leaders. Strauss and Howe define the Boomer generation as anyone who doesn't personally remember World War II. They almost had to be very different from the Silent Generation, who shared the formative experience of having a childhood during the war. The Prophet-Boomers grow up as protected children during a High and never personally experience a Crisis Period until they were elders. As the moralistic, uncompromising young adult crusaders of an Awakening Period – remember the '60s? – they were likely to start an Unraveling Period when they become Midlifers in control of our country's institutions, and they did. That is followed by a Crisis Period, *which is right where we are today.*

The table below from Strauss and Howe shows how these cycles have played out for the last 500+ years:

Generation	Type	Birth Years	Description
Late Medieval Cycle			
Arthurian Generation	Hero (Civic)	1433–1460	
Humanist Generation	Artist (Adaptive)	1461–1482	
Reformation Cycle			
Reformation Generation	Prophet (Idealist)	1483–1511	
Reprisal Generation	Nomad (Reactive)	1512–1540	
Elizabethan Generation	Hero (Civic)	1541–1565	
Parliamentarian Generation	Artist (Adaptive)	1566–1587	
New World Cycle			
Puritan Generation	Prophet (Idealist)	1588–1617	
Cavalier Generation	Nomad (Reactive)	1618–1647	
Glorious Generation	Hero (Civic)	1648–1673	
Enlightenment Generation	Artist (Adaptive)	1674–1700	
Revolutionary Cycle			
Awakening Generation	Prophet (Idealist)	1701–1723	

Liberty Generation	Nomad (Reactive)	1724–1741	The First Great Awakening, a period of heightened religious activity
Republican Generation	Hero (Civic)	1742–1766	
Compromise Generation	Artist (Adaptive)	1767–1791	
Civil War Cycle			
Transcendental Generation	Prophet (Idealist)	1792–1821	
Gilded Generation	Nomad (Reactive)	1822–1842	Awakening, a period of great religious revival with widespread Christian evangelism and conversions.
Progressive Generation	Artist (Adaptive)	1843–1859	This is the only Cycle where a generational cohort was skipped – there was no Hero generation.
Great Power Cycle			
Missionary Generation	Prophet (Idealist)	1860–1882	
Lost Generation	Nomad (Reactive)	1883–1900	The Third Great Awakening, a period of religious activism that affected pietistic Protestant denominations and had a strong sense of social activism.

G.I. Generation	Hero (Civic)	1901–1924	
Silent Generation	Artist (Adaptive)	1925–1942	
Millennial Cycle			
Baby Boom Generation	Prophet (Idealist)	1943–1960	
Generation X	Nomad (Reactive)	1961–1981	Shaped by six influences: Readily-accessible birth control; legalization of abortion on demand; increase in divorce; increase in mothers in the work place; the Zero Population movement and "Devil-child films."
Millennial Generation	Hero (Civic)	1982–2000	Many in this cohort grew up during the rapid growth of technology and economic and social globalization.
New Silent Generation	Artist (Adaptive)	2001–2021(?)	This generation is the first to be born in a digital world and are currently in grade school.

Can Chairman Bernanke and the Fed print enough money to neutralize the Crisis Period that began in 2001? No. This period must play out until 2021, with the Baby Boomer Prophets as the wise elders to provide a bridge to the coming High Period. The Boomers hold the ideals of the High Period and Awakening Period, and their job is to keep reminding everyone that the hard times will pass and the country will get back to a positive, uplifting period of great advances. Some will deride them as sentimental old fools, but fortunately they never cared much what other people thought of them.

The midlifers in control during the Crisis Period are Generation X. Like all previous Nomad generations, the cynicism and coping skills they developed as under-protected children give them the toughness and street-smarts to lead during a crisis. Ben Bernanke was born in 1953, virtually in the middle of the baby boom. But President Obama and Secretary of the Treasury Tim Geithner were born in 1961, either at the end of the baby boom as it is conventionally counted or the beginning of Generation X, as Strauss and Howe count it. Either way, they have a foot in both worlds, with some of the moralistic hope of the boomers and some of the cynical street-smarts of the Gen Xers. I think at some point they are likely to dump or marginalize Bernanke, probably after some serious manifestation of the Crisis Period makes it clear the game has changed and Alan Greenspan's policies won't work anymore.

Greenspan was born in 1926, a Silent Generation, indecisive, adaptive Artist capable of leading during the Awakening Period to 1981, but the wrong man for the job during the Unraveling Period that began after inflation was beaten, from 1982 through the dotcom crash. The Fed needed a moralistic Baby Boomer leader who would say something was wrong and then take steps to stop it, not an adaptive Artist willing to go along, avoid judgments and try to make everything work smoothly together. By facilitating a string of bubbles in the economy, the stock market, emerging economies and the real estate market, Greenspan helped engineer what Harry Dent titled one of his books: *The Roaring 2000s*. And like The Roaring '20s that it echoed, it preceded powerful deflationary forces in the economy that are made much worse by the prior boom.

So now, when the generational cycle calls for a cynical, street-smart Generation Xer to pick up the pieces from the Unraveling Period and lead us through the Crises Period, we have a baby boomer running the Fed. Wrong guy, wrong time, wrong place.

The second great deflationary force, generational economics, eventually will overwhelm whatever Bernanke tries to do. But that will come only after Bernanke has given his all to stop deflation, including tanking the dollar and risking hyperinflation.

The Consumer Credit Implosion

The idea that the credit implosion has a big generational component may be new to you, but the fact of the implosion should be obvious. When I graduated from college, almost no one had a student loan that had to be paid back. Some of us had a military obligation because there were ways to sign up for ROTC, collect a stipend while in college, and then do a relatively small amount of additional training to become a second lieutenant and spend three or four years in the service. I recall a study that said the half-life of a second lieutenant in combat was seven seconds, but try telling that to an 18-year-old.

Then along came the student loan programs, Pell grants and such, and students were able to borrow to afford much higher tuitions. So colleges raised tuitions at a rate much higher than the general inflation rate, transferring large amounts of government-guaranteed money to themselves while leaving the students the obligation to pay it back. All of a sudden, students started graduating with very large debt burdens, especially those who had to go to graduate school to pursue their careers in medicine, law, banking, teaching and so on.

GenXers and the Millennials hate student loan debt, which keeps them living poor for years, and have learned to hate all debt.

They all have friends who piled some auto or credit card debt on top of the student loans, and now are being hounded by debt collectors – often government debt collectors. The Fed can't push their credit string at the Baby Boomers, who are downsizing for retirement. Aging baby boomers are long past their peak spending years, and more interested in getting out of debt than adding to it to fund bigger houses, college tuitions, new cars and buying crap destined for the landfill just to keep up with the neighbors. And the Fed can't push their credit string at the GenXers, who are suspicious of more debt. So some of the financial engineering their parents relied on, like subprime mortgages and the home equity ATM, are no longer wanted or needed, shrinking and possibly disappearing. That makes this a *generational* credit implosion, and we won't see the kind of easy credit use that the Fed would like to see for another 20 or 40 years. Conspicuous consumption has been replaced by calculated consumption.

Yet the most obvious of the three deflationary forces the Fed is fighting is the credit implosion. It probably is the only one they see, and as it garners most of the headlines and occupies most of the Fed's time. Because it is the only financially-based of the deflationary forces, it also must seem to Bernanke to be the one that he *should* be working on, because he has some tools. Finally, it is a really big problem. This is the worst credit-based deflation since the Great Depression

Because the credit-fueled boom lasted so long, there is a lot of adjusting to do, beginning with a dramatic adjustment in real housing prices back to their long-term trend level. Housing prices increased much faster than inflation in the '80s and '90s, and the adjustment back to trend level is happening quickly and painfully. Going forward, in a significant inflation or, especially, hyperinflation one would expect house prices to increase like any other asset denominated in dollars. Even though it might not quite keep up with inflation, real estate is a good hedge against inflation. Of course, to the extent that future mortgage rates reflect future inflation, the housing market eventually will grind to a halt due to high nominal rates. We saw that happen when then-Fed Chairman Paul Volker threw on the clamps in 1980.

Outside of housing, there has been a significant build-up in private debt, primarily for credit cards and long-term automobile financing. This is an individual problem in the early stages, as families here and there get overextended. The banking industry pushed through much stricter bankruptcy laws when they saw this problem developing. Now the bankruptcy judge must consider an applicant's last six months of income, even if the precipitating reason they are filing Chapter 11 is that they lost their job and don't have the income any more. Credit counseling is required to be sure the applicant can't repay his or her debts under a Chapter 13 restructuring program. No repeat bankruptcy is allowed for eight years. All of an applicant's turnips are put in a vise to see if any blood can be squeezed out of them, and debtors are sent to prison…no, wait, those provisions didn't make it into the final bill, in spite of the banking lobbyists.

These individual problems become a systemic problem when everyone is doing it. Are people who run a negative savings rate just dumb, or are they wise enough to see the hyperinflation and breakdown that is coming, and simply buying assets now with money that will become worthless? High inflation reduces the real debt load of consumers just as effectively as that of governments. The bankers who tightened the bankruptcy noose may catch a few people who can't stay afloat until the Great Inflation kicks in, but after that they get paid back easily with ever-more-worthless dollars.

The Government Credit Explosion

Of course, individual unsecured debt is not a patch on government debt. The Fed seems determined to offset the consumer credit implosion with a Federal government credit explosion, chanting the classical mantra that if consumer demand wavers, it must be replaced by government demand to soften or avoid a downturn in the economy. The expansion of the Federal Reserve's balance sheet, composed of overpriced or toxic assets offset by real liabilities, has been sensational. The annual Federal budget deficit is at levels that were inconceivable just three to five years ago, with the targeted faith-based reductions getting back to levels that are still breathtaking. The unfunded Social Security, Medicare, Medicaid and state and Federal pension obligations are impossible to honor in real terms. Their terms will be altered with much later retirements and means testing, and then even if the nominal dollar obligations are met, inflation will dramatically reduce the real benefits.

What Mismanagement in Washington Has Done

Here is the ugly truth about profligacy, American style, with my best estimates of the huge amount of debt Washington and Wall Street are dumping on the American taxpayer and their children, with thanks to Paul Farrell of MarketWatch, who started me looking at the individual categories. First, the overall problem is that total U.S. debt, including banking liabilities, has soared relative to economic growth over the past 20 years. (See chart next page)

1. Federal government debt ... $14.3 trillion

The Federal debt has *doubled* since 2005 to $14.3 trillion, due in large part to two unnecessary wars and numerous stimulus programs designed to save incompetent institutions that needed to be liquidated. Expect Federal debt to increase at $1 trillion to $1.5 trillion a year for at least the next 10 years. About $5 trillion is now owned by foreigners, who are adding about $400 billion a year until they get tired of us vacuuming up all their cash.

2. Treasury and Fed cheap-money policies ... $23.7 trillion

Until and if we get a Fed audit, we'll never know for sure where our money is going. The Fed's electronic printing presses have created an estimated $23.7 trillion in credits, grants, loans and guarantees, backed by you and your kids. Sorry, they won't tell you who got it.

3. Social Security unfunded commitment ... $40 trillion

Cut benefits? Raise taxes 40%? Means-test benefits? Sharply raise the retirement age? Delays in fixing Social Security limit the choices and worsen the solution, but Congress does nothing so well as kick the can down the road. By 2035, Social Security and Medicare will eat up the entire federal budget, other than defense. Washington's response: Heck, let them worry about it.

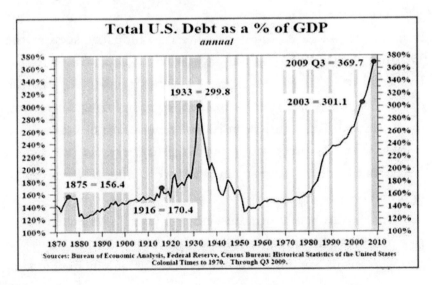

Total U.S. Debt as a % of GDP
annual

2009 Q3 = 369.7
1933 = 299.8
2003 = 301.1
1875 = 156.4
1916 = 170.4

Sources: Bureau of Economic Analysis, Federal Reserve, Census Bureau: Historical Statistics of the United States Colonial Times to 1970. Through Q3 2009.

Of course, almost everyone realizes there is nothing in the Social Security "trust fund." In 1995, Senator Diane Feinstein (D-CA) responded to an opponent's TV commercial by saying: "No amount of self-financed television commercials is going to stop me from fighting to protect the Social Security Trust Fund." That's probably the last time anyone tried to pretend there was something of value in the "trust fund" worth protecting.

The Social Security program is a promise to pay benefits to those who contribute, with specific rules on when and how much benefit will be paid. The excess money that was paid into Social Security was simply spent by the government. Worse, when they took it from the trust fund they counted it as income to make the annual Federal deficit look smaller. That's right, Bill Clinton did not run a real surplus in his last year in office. It was an accounting gimmick worthy of an Enron – borrow money and call it revenues.

In exchange for taking it, the government "gave" Social Security an I.O.U. saying they promised to pay it back so it could be used to pay benefits. *But the government had already promised to pay the benefits.* If the money had been kept separate and invested in a very broad-based index of American industry, such as the Wilshire 3000 Index, it could have provided capital for productive activities that earned income and built value towards the day those who paid it retired. Instead, by spending it the government created a tax burden on future generations of workers – a burden that will prove to be too large to carry. So the system will default on its promises in real terms, and maybe even in nominal terms.

Will the cost-of-living adjustment (COLA) save Social Security recipients from raging inflation? Let's put it this way: The guy who has to pay out more money is the same guy in charge of calculating the index that says how much more money he has to pay out. The temptation to mess with the Consumer Price Index has to be overwhelming. And at this point there is a great deal of history and precedent for messing with it. The deviation from the traditional CPI started under Ronald Reagan, and really hit its stride under Bill Clinton. If house prices are exploding and rents are rising much slower, then substitute rental equivalents for prices in the Index. So many of these little adjustments have been done that the current CPI Index deviates rather dramatically from the one that was used up until the Reagan years. I am not saying the old index was more or less accurate than the new one, but rather that the government can change it when they want to, for any reason they want to. Here is a comparison between the government number, CPI-U, and the SGS Alternative CPI from ShadowStats.com:

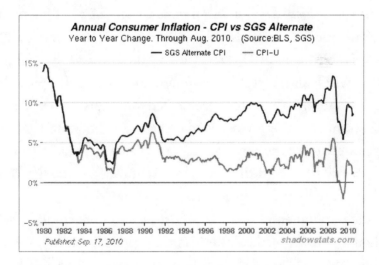

4. Medicare unfunded commitment... $60 trillion

Going broke faster than Social Security, so requires a harder kick. Hey, here's an idea. This is a big problem calling for big solutions, right? So whatever the solution is down the road, it should be big enough to cover even more benefits. So let's pass a prescription-drug benefit – it only adds an unfunded $8.1 trillion. In 2005 the estimated unfunded commitment was $35 trillion. Add the $8.1 trillion and that gets us to today's estimate of $43.1...I mean $60 trillion. It's D.C. accounting, what can I say? Kicking this ballooning can very far down the road requires an expert kicker. Maybe John Carney will retire from football and run for Congress.

5. Global real estate losses ... $15 trillion

Commercial and residential real estate loans are 25% of U.S. bank balance sheets. "Mark to market" has been replaced by "mark to fantasy" accounting. An unknown amount of the most toxic assets have been transferred to the Fed's balance sheet, already included in #2, above.

6. State and local budget and pension shortfalls ... $3.5 trillion

State budget shortfalls will total around $110 billion in 2010, and $180 billion in 2011. Don't worry, the Fed and the Administration will loan the states the money to avoid bankruptcy. That means these shortfalls will become Federal assets...whoa, a shortfall becomes an asset? Yes, a loan on the Fed's books to California is an asset, even though California will never be able to pay it back. Someday, down the road (kick that can!), some future Fed Chairman will write off the loan.

State public employee pension plans are underfunded by $3 trillion according to the American Enterprise Institute for Public Policy Research. The states claim they are only $438 billion underfunded, because they assume that can earn high returns with no risk. (hahahahaha.) Add more than $450 billion in annual shortfalls in local government employee pension funds, as far as the eye can see.

7. *Corporate pensions plans underfunded ... $200 billion*

About 92% of corporate pension plans are underfunded, with the average shortfall at about 15%. Any defaults are guaranteed by taxpayers via the Pension Benefit Guaranty Corporation.

8. *Consumer card debt ... $2.5 trillion and holding*

Even during the downturn and including the defaults, consumer debt rose from about $2.3 trillion to $2.5 trillion. It now seems to be flattening out as the GenXers and Millennials turn away from Shylock interest rates.

9. *International sovereign debt*

The U.S. dollar is still the world's reserve currency, and the Chinese yuan is formally pegged to the dollar, while the euro is informally backed by the dollar through Bernanke's unlimited dollar/euro swap facility, The coming U.S. inflation/hyperinflation will quickly morph into a world inflation/hyperinflation. This is not Zimbabwe making a joke of themselves, or Argentina deciding to walk away from their debt. This is the biggest economy in the world with the world's reserve currency circling the drain.

Most countries will not be able to cushion themselves from the impact. The big holders of U.S. dollars – Japan, China and Russia – get slammed directly. In the rest of the world, national governments will issue about $4.5 trillion in debt this year, about triple the average for the last five years. (See chart next page)

The world's governments are leveraging up together, which means the cushion against a financial accident is getting thinner and thinner, if it still exists at all. Most of this debt is being issued at extraordinarily low, controlled interest rates. When rates rise, as they must, national budgets will be slammed far beyond the ability of already-burdened taxpayers to cover the increase. And when one must borrow money to pay the interest – well, that is

2010 Projected Sovereign Debt Issuance

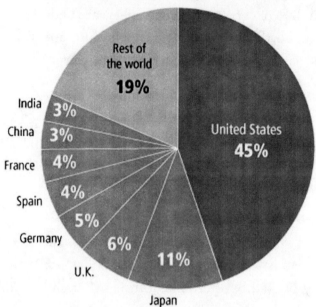

Sources: IMF World Economic Outlook and other various public sources, including
news media and respective government data; Hayman Advisors estimates.

why GM went broke and why GE is going to follow them. Once interest starts compounding against you, it's over, Greece being the latest example.

In *This Time It's Different: Eight Centuries of Financial Folly*, Carmen Reinhart and Kenneth Rogoff found that once a developed economy goes beyond a 90% ratio of government debt to GDP, growth rates drop two percentage points lower, on average, than economies that have not yet crossed the line. The U.S. government-debt-to-GDP ratio is 84%, and both parties seem committed to policies that will drive it higher. The Feds have to sell nearly $2.5 trillion of debt in 2010 to cover the massive budget deficit and refund maturing paper, easily the largest amount in history. Pile on top of that billions more in offerings from states and municipalities, all bleeding money. By the end of 2010, total Federal, state and municipal government debt will shoot up to a stunning 350% of GDP. At some point, the market runs out of real buyers, and either the Fed inflates its balance sheet even faster by taking down the debt (rock), or long bond yields will begin their inexorable climb to new record highs, exceeding the Volker era (hard place).

The Congressional Budget Office assumptions about future budget deficits are based on the historic growth rate of 4%, not the 2% predicted by Reinhart and Rogoff's data. So excessive debt depresses growth, and then low growth increases deficits and makes paying down the debt an impossible job. Creditors get nervous and insist on higher rates on new and rolled-over debt, increasing the deficits even further and making it obvious the debt can never be paid down. Rating agencies cut from AAA to AA or A, and the cost of debt goes even higher, making the deficits bigger yet. Vicious circle, anyone?

The credit default swap market is pricing in a 3.1% chance of default during the next five years on U.S. Treasury debt. That's up from a 0.1% chance not that long ago. In addition to the possibility of a default from the top down starting in the U.S., which sells 45% of its debt to foreigners, the world has to worry about a default starting in a smaller country like Greece or Ireland, and then having a domino effect through the global banking system that brings down the U.S. The late Citibank chairman Walter Wriston, who almost lost the bank twice during one oil bust and one South American financial crisis, famously said that "countries don't go bankrupt."

Oh, yes, they do. Argentina, Brazil and Guatemala all defaulted, Argentina twice in the last 25 years. Zimbabwe has effectively defaulted through hyperinflation of their currency. Iceland probably will default; they have refused to pay $5 billion to British and Dutch savers in their busted banks. Ireland or Greece should pull out of the Eurozone and default, and Greece might actually do it because the citizenry shows little tolerance for a decade of austerity.

Sovereign defaults often follow global financial crises, wars or the boom and bust of commodities:

The Bank for International Settlements (BIS) says European and American banks have $1.7 trillion of debt issued by Portugal, Ireland, Italy, Greece and Spain. Germany and France have the biggest exposure, between them, holding more than $900 billion of PIIGS debt. German banks alone hold $45 billion and French banks hold a whopping $75 billion. No wonder French President Nicolas Sarkozy was practically beating his shoe on the table to get German Chancellor Angela Merkel to agree to bail out Greece. If she hadn't, he would have had to bail out his own banks with no money to do it. Plus, he needs the precedent in case France hits the wall.

Deleverage, De Sooner, De Better

Add all the above together, and it is clear that the world has to deleverage. There is simply too much debt to have a stable economic system, or to ever pay back. Deleveraging can be done by dramatically increasing the savings rate and taxes, and retiring debt. Or it can be done by renegotiating terms, or by default. All of those are very deflationary, creating hard times that not only hurt the average citizen but, far worse from a politician's point of view, cause incumbents to lose elections.

But for countries with control of their currency, like the U.S. and the U.K. – and I would include the Eurozone as a "country" here – deleveraging can be done by inflation. The debt doesn't go away, but it gets paid back with ever-less-valuable dollars. People on fixed incomes get hurt, bondholders who don't hedge get hurt, but the average Joe's income goes up every year while his mortgage and car payments stay the same, so he's happy. And happy constituents re-elect incumbents.

CHAPTER 5

The Third Force: Technology Everywhere

MOORE'S LAW TRUMPS KEYNES *AND* FRIEDMAN

*Human felicity is produced not as much
by great pieces of good fortune that seldom happen
as by little advantages that occur every day.*
—Benjamin Franklin

Technology is the third great deflationary force loose in our economy and the world. It is also the least recognized and understood, and the idea that its effects can be countered by fiscal or monetary policy is ludicrous. But because it is only dimly recognized as one cause of the current economic hardship, it is not surprising that inappropriate policies are used to offset it.

The quick take here is that the New Economy touted during the dotcom era is here. Not only did the idea not die with Pets.com and Webvan, it has come to dominate the world. There were many cries of joy and relief when the dotcom stocks crashed, as it "proved" that people like me and George Gilder were extremist nuts. There was no funnier denouncement than the one from a perpetually dour Parisian who essentially said the whole New Economy thing was a hoax – in a daily email sent to 300,000 people over the Internet, at zero marginal cost.

Even though he might not have realized in 2001 how much the world was about to change, I'll bet he does now. Technology has flattened business, allowing companies to communicate and manage processes essentially for free. Now they can design in the U.S., write code in Romania, produce in China, sell a name brand all over the world, find customers over the Internet and do customer service from India. For any given quality, technology allows them to dramatically lower costs, and *lower costs = lower prices = deflation*.

Moore's Law

Gordon Moore, a founder of Intel, propounded Moore's Law. It says that the number of transistors incorporated in a chip will approximately double every 24 months. Moore's Law implies that the cost of doing anything with a semiconductor falls about 50% every 24 months. This is because the semiconductor equipment manufacturers and chipmakers reduce the feature size – the width of the circuit lines – at the same pace. It costs about the same amount of money to process a semiconductor wafer on the new equipment as it did on the old, but about twice as many chips can be fit on each wafer. The result is an ever-increasing number of transistors per square inch, and can be seen in a chart of Intel's processors. (See chart on next page)

Metcalfe's Law

Bob Metcalfe, the inventor of Ethernet, propounded Metcalfe's Law, which says that the value of a telecommunications network

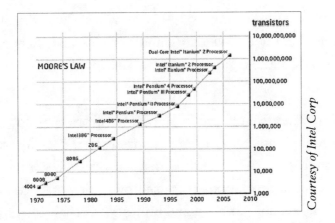

Courtesy of Intel Corp

is proportional to the *square* of the number of connected users of the system. (Although this Law was popularized by George Gilder in 1993, he attributed it to Bob.) It turns out that the costs of using a networked system may fall even faster than Moore's Law dictates for semiconductors. As a corollary to both laws, the cost of using wireless spectrum has fallen steadily since the time of Marconi (who did not invent the radio, incidentally, see km5kg. com/marconi.htm).

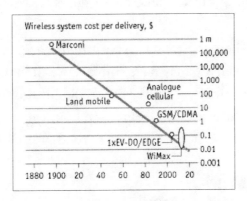

To put the magnitude of this revolution in perspective, I am going to quote at length some excerpts from the third edition of *Every Investor's Guide to High Tech Stocks and Mutual Funds*, a book I wrote in 1996 that was first published by Broadway Books

(Random House) in January 1997. You will see why the Fed trying to counteract the deflationary impact of technology change ranks with King Canute trying to hold back the tide.

* * * * *

Economies usually evolve slowly, but from time to time they go through a rapid, wrenching change that creates massive, new opportunities at the same time that old structures are destroyed. Each of these revolutions is caused by the emergence of a new, underlying economic driver, and brings with it new infrastructures that change society. We are living through one of those major changes right now, and it is creating once in a lifetime opportunities to build new wealth.

When you are living through it, it can be difficult to put it in perspective. But 10,000 years back, your great-great-great-great-granddaddy[10] was a hunter-gatherer. The economic driver was meat protein. Always on the move, taking what food and shelter he found along the way, our distant ancestor rarely deferred current consumption to make investments that would pay off in the future.

Not that there were many investment choices. Great-grand-daddy[10] and his mate may have smoked or salted meat to save for the winter, but that was pretty much the limit of their ability to invest for the future. They didn't build wealth, and there wasn't much of an infrastructure – little beyond animal trails through the woods.

The Agrarian Society

Then – paradigm shift! – life evolved to an agrarian society where your great-grandparents[8] farmed the land, saved seeds for next year's crop, developed water systems, and built houses. Towns sprung up to market crops and provide a center to buy supplies. The agrarian society lasted for thousands of years – until 300 years ago, give or take.

What drove wealth building in this new society was land and crops. If you owned the land, you were wealthy. If not, not. The enabling technology was pretty much limited to hand tools and horses. The infrastructure constituted of dirt roads and couriers on horseback.

The United States was discovered and settled towards the end of this period. Having a limitless supply of land, lots of water, and not many regulations, the pioneers built great wealth rapidly. (Hong Kong did the same thing over the last 50 years on only 400 square miles, so we know that land isn't the issue anymore.)

The Industrial Revolution

Then came the Industrial Revolution, driven by cheap steel and a flood of new inventions. Wealth grew in steel, industrial machinery, coal, and transportation. The infrastructure changed to railroads, shipping, and the telegraph. The important economic indicators shifted to coal, iron and steel production, patent applications, and railroad operating income.

Great family fortunes were built in these new areas – glittering names, still well known, such as Morgan, Bessemer, Vanderbilt, Astor. Although investors could still make money buying and selling in the agrarian economy, it was much easier to get the wind at their backs and investing in the new areas side-by-side with the entrepreneurs.

But they weren't dubbed "entrepreneurs" in those days. They were called "robber barons."

The Mass-Production Economy

After World War I, the United States and most of the developed world shifted to mass-production and consumer-based economies, thanks, in some measure, to Henry Ford. The economic driver changed to cheap energy – especially oil. The middle class grew faster, with enough income and an enabling technology (the automobile) to move out of the noisy, polluted cities. People did not have to live within walking distance of the factory anymore.

At that point, the growth industries changed to autos, housing, and retail. The infrastructure shifted to highways, airports, telephones, and broadcasting. The important economic indicators changed to retail sales, auto sales, housing starts, and capacity utilization.

Again great new family fortunes were built in these areas. Automobile families were the royalty of the Midwest; home building created many multimillionaires after World War II. The Walton (Wal-Mart) success story may be the last example of that era. Again, investors earned the highest returns by focusing on rapid growth areas in the economy.

The Technology Economy

As with all generalizations, it's easy to argue about when the Digital Age began. Mainframe computers went commercial in the 1950s; Digital Equipment Corporation was founded in 1957. But it was the demands of the Department of Defense plus NASA that drove the process of miniaturization to the point where Fairchild and Texas Instruments invented the semiconductor. And Intel, descendant of Fairchild, gave birth to the microprocessor in 1971.

Microprocessors powered the digital watches and handheld calculators of the mid-1970s. By the late 1970s, personal computers were spreading by the tens of thousands. Apple computers could even be seen on the desks of non-wonks in ordinary companies.

But this was not yet the Age of Empowerment, when anyone could own a personal computer for less than $5,000 and make it do useful things. It took IBM to put the Good Housekeeping seal of approval on personal computers by coming out with its own in 1981, clearly marking the latest change in the economy.

Now there's no question: This is the technology economy, and the economic driver is ever-cheaper semiconductors. Underlying all the advances in computing and communications are unbelievable price drops in semiconductor chips. Moore's Law has been right thus far, and I expect it will continue to hold true for the next 10 years at least, at which time the physical limitations of silicon may force a rethinking of the whole technology. But you never know. Twenty years ago, it was thought that microprocessors could never go faster than 100-megahertz. Now you can buy 3000-megahertz Intel processors (3 gigahertz), and people are waiting impatiently for faster models.

The growth industries in the new economy are computers, software, semiconductors, communications, the Internet, and medical technology, and the infrastructure is changing to satellites, fiber optics, networks, and wireless connectivity. Again the great new family fortunes are being dealt built in these areas – just ask Bill Gates, Larry Ellison or Sergey Brin.

So how do we measure this?

Of course, the relevant economic indicators have changed again. It's just that the government and the media haven't quite figured it out.

We used to get 10 day auto-sales figures; where are 10-day smartphone-sales figures?

Why don't we hear about the high-tech trade balance (which shows a multibillion-dollar surplus)?

How about knowledge-intensive employment, which grew rapidly through many recession and continues to show lower-than-average unemployment? Of the U.S. regions with the fastest job growth in the early 1990s, San Jose and San Francisco (at either end of Silicon Valley) were first and third.

How about the *de*flation in high-tech prices, which drop reliably every year? One hundred megabytes of hard-disk drive storage cost $250 in 1988, $35 in 1994, and $2.50 in 2000. It now costs less than half a cent.

Year after year, technology companies grow about 15% with no inflation, while the rest of the economy plods along at 2% to 3% real growth. Although technology started as a small, specialized segment of the economy in the 1970s, after several years of rapid relative growth, the new technology economy accounts for almost 20% of the total economy.

Well, 20% times 15% is 3% growth. That's real GDP growth of 3% per year from the technology sector alone, no matter what the Federal Reserve Board does.

Yet, once we get in a recovery cycle, the Fed, in its wisdom, will not allow the total economy to grow faster than 4%. That means the acceptable growth rate for the entire non-technology economy is 1%. Worse, the mass-production and consumer economy is saddled with debt, running a huge trade deficit in oil and automobiles, and suffering low growth due to the demographics of aging baby boomers. No wonder people are feeling financially stressed!

In this foot-on-the-brake environment, investors should be bailing out of the old mass-production economy, not to mention the even older industrial economy. (The latter is extremely vulnerable to foreign competition from the newly industrializing countries.) There should be a rush to align investment capital with the new entrepre-neurial areas – especially in the United States. Except for robotics, where Japan is first, the United States dominates the new technology economy. The two top personal-computer manufacturers are U.S. companies. Now that technology markets have expanded to include consumers as well as corporations, and the entire world – instead of just the United States, Europe, and Japan – U.S. dominance of most technology industries could produce domestic wealth comparable to Britain's in the Industrial Revolution of the 1880s.

R&D

The real driver for long-term technology profits is the research-and-development programs that create future earnings. Why is R&D such a powerful economic driver? Information and knowl-edge are the essence of any economy. In the agrarian economy, knowledge was passed along orally and recorded in a few books and journals. The industrial and mass-production economies added blueprints, magazines, newspapers, and inexpensive books. In a technology economy, information is also gathered in databases that reflect the experience and know-how of millions of people, networked to the data and to each other. The knowledge explosion is both the cause and the effect of technological progress.

Information gets into the economy primarily by lowering costs (deflation). Real costs always fall. That is, adjusted for inflation, the real cost of creating something is under constant competitive pressure. This is the definition of productivity, and the direct cause of an increasing standard of living. Yet it is misinterpreted by the Fed as deflation that might lead to a depression, and caused them to try to fight the effects of technology on prices – a Don Quixote mission at best.

"Learning-curve" economics is best illustrated by the semi-conductor industry. Since 1970, the cost of manufacturing one bit of random access memory has fallen 28% per year. By increasing wafer sizes, shrinking transistor sizes, and improving production equipment continually, semiconductor companies make the same profit today as they did 20 years ago – on much larger sales. Now the cost of memory, processing and communications is so low that demand has exploded and it is used to improve hundreds of low-priced ordinary consumer goods.

Virtually all the net growth in the economy will come from technology: electronics technology, entertainment technology, communications technology, technology exports, new medical technology, and biotechnology drugs. Investors in technology are buying into inevitably superior long-term performance. At the same time, we are in the midst of one of the occasional periods of surging technological change. The economy is adapting to new technologies, new consumer demands, new cost structures, and new educational needs. Retraining workers is a political battle cry. The combination of a rising long wave of growth and a high rate of technological change will bring about a radical economic and social transformation, providing extraordinary investment opportunities.

The fall of communism added over two billion people to the world's labor and consumer force. The internationalization of the world economy will intensify competition, forcing all companies to use the latest technology. Thus, high rates of economic growth will have a worldwide impact.

Technology companies tend to sell worldwide, with 20% to 70% of sales overseas. No matter how fast the United States grows, we can be sure that Latin America and the industrializing Pacific Rim will grow faster. Europe may struggle with lower growth due to its high-cost, social-welfare economies, and Japan may be fighting a depression for many years. But most of the world is a wonderful market for U.S. exporters; first among them are the technology companies.

If you want the investment winds at your back, you must invest in technology. The old days of "growth" by raising prices are over. Technology companies cut prices each year; technology managements know how to manage for growth in a deflation – they've never known any other environment. These are the managers for the 21st century.

But we'll take companies growing 15% to 50% a year with no debt, shipping 20% to 70% of their products overseas, investing 7% to 20% of sales in R&D to invent new products that create sales growth and carry high profit margins to boot. During the next six years the cost of computing will fall by 90%. The Mobile Internet Device market will nearly triple. Communications traffic will increase by a factor of five. There'll be at least another double in Internet accounts. Almost 200 biotechnology drugs will be approved by the Food & Drug Administration, many to treat previously untreatable chronic diseases of aging that cost the health-care system billions of dollars every year. It is indeed the best of times to be a technology investor – regardless of what Ben Bernanke does.

What is The Market Telling Us?

Although the change to a technology economy is 35 years under way, historical reliance on economic indicators from the mass-production and commodity economies is fooling industry and government. At the end of 1996, Federal Reserve Chairman Alan Greenspan finally said:

"While there can be little doubt that major gains are being made in today's market in the quality, choice, and availability of goods and services for American consumers, it is also clear that we measure these trends rather poorly. First, there are questions about the quality of the data we employ to measure output in today's economy. Second, like the major technological advances of earlier periods, it will take time for our newest innovations to work their way into the nation's infrastructure in a productive manner.

In the computer software industry, for example, what is the price per unit and how does that price move from one period to the next? Also, we know that if we are expending an increasing proportion of our gross domestic product denominated in current dollars on medical services. But what is the physical equivalent unit of output of medical care? What is the true price trend for the removal of cataracts, when the technology and the nature of the whole procedure is so dramatically different from what it was, say, 40 or even 20 years ago?"

The Take-Home Message

The Fed is not setting policy in light of the realities of a technology economy. If the Fed is threatened by prices falling, they are doomed because *they don't understand the difference between a deflation and a depression.* The U.S. economy was in a general deflation from 1873 to 1896 due to the rapid introduction of Industrial Revolution technology, yet the economy was just fine. The Great Sag or The Great Deflation, as this period is known, was a global deflation possibly started by a return to the gold standard after the Civil War. Because it persisted due to the introduction of cost-cutting and productivity-enhancing technologies, it baffled the experts and resisted all attempts by the politicians to reverse it. According to Milton Friedman, prices fell 1.7% a year in the United States and 0.8% a year in Britain for a generation.

In a deflation, saving is encouraged because your dollars will be worth more tomorrow than today. Living standards rise because things are getting cheaper, and if that is happening due to technology then productivity is improving and the standard of living goes up, not down. Of course, it is hard on debtors who have to pay back their debts in stronger and stronger dollars, but widespread recognition that we are in deflation causes consumers and companies to change their behavior to avoid debt. There is only one entity that will not avoid debt: The Federal Government. Having the best Congress money can buy means profligate, unnecessary spending will be with us until taxpayers demand a radical overhaul of the political pork system.

Not understanding the impact of technology as a deflationary force can lead to some ludicrous situations. For example, President Obama has said that his $8 billion stimulus spending for some high-speed rail lines is just a down payment on a plan to build a complete high-speed rail network, drawing comparisons to the 1950s creation of the interstate highway system. Congress is working on proposals that would expand high-speed rail, including one plan that would spend $50 billion over the next five years. Presumably, they are doing this to improve productivity by moving goods faster and attracting people to take a train instead of their car. Setting aside the issue of whether it will do that, if it succeeds it will *lower costs.* Oh, no! Deflation!! Better print some more money (???).

Just as in the Roaring Twenties, when the standard of living increased as new technologies like the automobile, radios, refrigerators and telephones became mainstream products, we are in a period when the standard of living could take another leap forward. True high-speed broadband Internet connections everywhere, instead of the silly facade of calling DSL "broadband," would provide the infra-structure for amazing new products and services. Nanotechnology is almost ready to come out of the labs and into production. The ability to create all-new materials with characteristics optimized for a particular use will unleash a tsunami of engineering creativity. Biotechnology, after years of heavy investment, is bringing great new drugs to market that actually treat the chronic diseases of aging, instead of trying to mask the symptoms.

But the Bernanke Fed's focus on solving the credit bubble problem of too much leverage to marginal borrowers by providing even *more* credit to even *more marginal* borrowers does not deal with the realities of aging baby boomer demographics, or the gener-ational change, or the impact of technology in a flat, wired world. Unfortunately, the policies the Fed is putting in place will badly weaken or possibly destroy the dollar, making the slim savings of the boomers worth less. Keeping prices artificially high will not replace the buying power of the boomers during their peak spending years. It damages the baby bust Generation X now coming into power, as well as the Millennials (echo baby boomers) to follow them, and guarantees that the Social Security fraud discussed in Chapter 4 will cause considerable intergenerational resentment.

Worst of all, a difficult or chaotic market for dollars as a store of value and the world's reserve currency could derail the R&D needed to fulfill the promise of the Internet, nanotechnology and biotechnology. Or the R&D still might happen, but in another country with a more stable currency that makes it possible to raise money, fund operations and pay people who want to do their work without having to run a wheelbarrow full of dollars to the store to buy bread. For the U.S., that would be the biggest tragedy of all – a potentially unrecoverable blow that starts the country down the historically familiar path to irrelevance, or even oblivion. I don't think the Bernanke Fed has any idea the risk they are taking by exploding the money supply and the Fed's balance sheet as a solution to problems that are rooted in demographics, generational change and falling costs due to the spread of technology.

PART III

The Bernanke Solution

Experience keeps a dear school,
but fools will learn in no other.
—Benjamin Franklin

CHAPTER 6

Destroy the Dollar?

*If you would know the value of money
try to borrow some.*
—Benjamin Franklin

Would the Fed deliberately destroy the dollar? Since they were founded in 1913, they have declared their two main jobs as acting to maintain an even economic keel by moderating the business cycle, and maintaining the value of the dollar. Here's how they've done on the dollar since their founding:

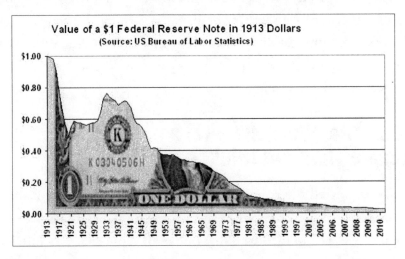

Value of a $1 Federal Reserve Note in 1913 Dollars
(Source: US Bureau of Labor Statistics)

The dollar has lost 95% of its value since the Fed was created. Yes, President Roosevelt confiscated gold in 1933 and then raised the price, and President Nixon cut the dollar free from gold in 1971. But you can bet in both cases the Fed was consulted and gave their blessing, at least behind the scenes.

The trouble with all currencies, gold-backed or fiat, is that the government is always tempted to debase them. A little inflation keeps the populace feeling like they are making progress, and with a progressive income tax system it gently lifts everyone into a higher average tax bracket, increasing the government's take.

Then, in a crisis like 2008, there are choices to be made. The answer to a crisis caused by excessive debt is to cut spending, tighten the belt, take the economic hit of a deep recession or depression, liquidate bankrupt entities, and clear the decks for a recovery. The trouble with that is that voters will kick everyone out of office who pursues those policies, and may riot in the streets (*cf.*, Greece).

The other choice is to run big deficits to ameliorate the downturn, use quantitative easing to buy government bonds and keep interest rates depressed, print money and make credit easy to get, and kick the can down the road. This works until the lenders to the government refuse to lend at artificially-depressed interest rates. At that point interest rates jump, blowing a hole in the budget that requires borrowing even more money at even higher rates, and a vicious downward circle ensues.

The Dollar Will Fall Faster & Sooner Than You Think

I committed the major no-no of giving away the conclusion of this section in the title, but bear with me for a bit. It's easy to say the dollar is a dead man walking, but as all those crowded into the bet against the dollar in January 2010 painfully learned, timing is indeed everything. Being short the dollar just as Greece's finances implode turned out to be a really bad bet. So why is the dollar, in the form of the current Federal Reserve notes, going to go away, and when, exactly, will the death spiral begin?

The dollar is going to die because very soon the U.S. government won't be able to pay the interest on its debt without borrowing more money. The government "earns" taxes and fees, but as the interest payments go up because (a) the debt keeps growing, and (b) lenders get credit qualms and raise rates, the government's interest payments will exceed its "earnings". At that point it has the same problem as Chrysler and General Motors had, or the next major corporate bankruptcy, General Electric. It has to borrow money to pay its interest, but every dollar it borrows reduces its credit quality a little bit *and* compounds against it, requiring even more borrowing in the future just to service the same original debt. It is not only a slippery slope, but an increasingly steep one. It is something like skiing down an intermediate slope that suddenly turns into an expert double black diamond run.

So the crucial number is the amount of government "earnings" required to pay the interest. The secondary numbers are the level and trend of "earnings" and interest. With some fairly simple assumptions, we can figure out when the buck will hit the fan.

Short term interest rates are abnormally low right now compared to long term rates, which also are low. The sensible thing to do if, for example, you have a mortgage is to refinance your adjustable rate into a low-interest fixed rate. That may seem hard to do on the surface, because your monthly payment will immediately go up, but in the long run you'll save your house.

If you are the government and need to cover the regular deficit, plus the stimulus program, plus two wars, plus the new health care initiative, the sensible thing to do is sell as much long-term debt as you can to lock in these low rates. So why has the U.S. Treasury moved more than half of the total U.S. debt into *short*-term notes? Because they aren't sensible and they don't think long-term. All they want to do is kick the can down the road and win President Obama a second term in 2012.

In the next two and a half years, to the end of 2012, they have us in a position where we have to roll over $4 trillion in existing debt, plus fund another probably $3.5 trillion in new debt to cover the expected deficits, and another $2.5 trillion for additional guarantees to the FDIC, Fannie Mae, Freddie Mac, the FHA and assorted other stimulus commitments. Normally, the holders of the existing $4 trillion would simply roll into the new paper as it becomes available. But the two biggest holders, China and Japan, are now *reducing* their holdings of U.S. debt. Both have questioned the credit quality of the U.S., the position of the dollar as the world's reserve currency, and the effectiveness of our stimulus programs in generating enough economic activity to make a dent in the new debt being created.

If the Treasury holds an auction in, say, 2011, and no one shows up, what happens? The Fed creates enough credit (dollars) to buy the debt. This is exactly like getting a new credit card to charge the interest on the old credit card – not do a balance transfer, just get new credit to make the minimum payments on the old credit. It only works if the dollar maintains its value, and that only happens if the foreign creditors are too dumb to see what is happening. But we know they already see what is happening, and they don't like it.

The World's Reserve Currency

The U.S. has gotten away with abnormally high trade deficits and domestic budget deficits for a long time because since World

War II the dollar has been the world's reserve currency, and we are the only country that can create dollars out of thin air. It's not only given us a huge financial free ride, but it's given us significant clout on the world stage, both economic and political. Some other countries that would like to be #1 have figured this out, and realized that if the dollar can be replaced by something else – most likely a basket of currencies that includes the dollar, euro, yuan and yen – then the political and economic power can be diffused and accrue to those who control the other currencies.

Thus, our good friends in Japan are pushing the Asian Region Currency Partnership, to be led and controlled by Japan, China and South Korea, which together produce 17% of the world's GDP. At 2009's trilateral Leader's Meeting and also at the Association of Southeast Asian Nations (ASEAN) discussions, regional financial cooperation was Topic #1. Japan's new prime minister said: "Until now we have been too reliant on the United States. I would like to develop policies that focus more on Asia." The Chinese prime minister said: "We have agreed to seek common ground and shelve our differences." Uh-oh.

And in the Middle East, OPEC has quite bluntly said they are tired of pricing oil in dollars and being jerked around when the dollar weakens against other currencies. They also are leaning towards a basket of currencies, and all it would take is setting up a trading market that settled transactions in the basket of currencies rather than the dollar. The basket undoubtedly would include the dollar, maybe as much as 25%, but also the euro, yuan, yen and – maybe – the ruble. Why the ruble? Because behind the scenes, Russia is supporting the basket idea, for obvious political reasons. So are China, Japan and France, again for obvious reasons that in China's case include expected rapid growth in the amount of petroleum they use every year. India and Brazil may sign on even if their currencies are not included. If the new trading exchange is located in London, even the Brits might be persuaded to back it. (But my friend Keith Fitz-Gerald of *Money Morning* thinks China wants the exchange located in Shanghai.)

The Numbers

Right now, our government "earns" about $1 trillion in income taxes plus about another $200 billion in import duties, fees and miscellaneous sources. They take in another $1 trillion from FICA and Medicare taxes, but they spend all that and more on Social Security and Medicare beneficiaries.

So the roughly $1.2 trillion in available "earnings" has to cover the costs of running the government and the military, plus pay interest on the debt. At the end of 2009, Federal on-balance sheet debt was about $11.8 trillion, and we paid about $445 billion in interest, or a measly average interest rate of 3.8%. By the end of 2012, the government will have about $18.5 trillion in debt, so even if the average interest rate does not rise, we will be paying $698 billion in interest. But we know the Fed has every intention of increasing interest rates as soon as possible to forestall inflation, and we know long rates are now low at 5%. If we assume the average interest rate increases to 5% as all the short-term debt is rolled over, which would still be below the Treasury's average interest rate for the last 30 years, then the annual interest goes to $925 million, or 92.5% of all the income taxes paid in fiscal 2009.

That doesn't leave a heck of a lot to pay the civil service and the military, not to mention funding all the payments for program commitments that already exist.

It is true that the economy will expand and tax revenues will increase by 2012, or at least we all hope so, but the interest payment burden is still far above any reasonable level. The rate of economic growth is uncertain, but the compounding interest from debt and deficits is mathematical. By 2012, long rates will be higher, too, and the Treasury will have lost its opportunity to lock in a 5% rate for decades. All this assumes our national credit quality does not take a huge hit on the world market, which is another heroic assumption.

Alan Greenspan, who never worried much about the tech bubble, the real estate bubble, or the effects of his 1% interest rate policy, now is warning about the disappearing: "large buffer between the level of our federal debt and our capacity to borrow. I'm finding it very difficult to look into the future and not worry about that."

I met with Marc Faber, the author of the *Gloom, Boom & Doom Report*, in Hong Kong in the mid-'90s, after we did some conference presentations together. He says this ends when our creditors lose confidence in our ability to ever get off the increasing debt treadmill. Payments on government debt suddenly go to 20%, 25% 30% of tax revenue. *Historically, once a country goes above 30%, it is done for.* It goes into default or the currency breaks down and the system collapses. The U.S. went above 20% in 2009, but instead of immediately cutting back, we seem dead-set on getting over 30% as quickly as possible. I think this happens on October 19, 2011 at 11:00am ET. So that is my forecast for when, exactly, the death spiral of the dollar will begin.

I'd love to be wrong about all this. No one wants to see millions of people wiped out and our country's economic power destroyed. But, sadly, that is our present course. Until something changes dramatically and soon, the prudent thing to do is to protect yourself by getting some of your assets out of the U.S. The easiest and first thing to do is to open a foreign bank account. Then buy real estate in a foreign country. Canada, Australia, New Zealand, Brazil, Uruguay, Paraguay, Argentina, Panama, Thailand – check them out, pick one and get started.

Greece: The Situation Is Hopeless But Not Serious (Unlike California, the U.K. and the U.S.)

Most of the weakness in the stock market in the second quarter of 2010 was due to concerns over the European Union's sovereign debt problems, especially in the quickly-acronymed PIIGS – Portugal, Ireland, Italy, Greece and Spain. Of these, Greece is in the most immediate trouble and has been the main focus of investor fears. Eurozone banks hold a lot of Greek debt, and the Greeks have been very good about creating large amounts of debt to maintain their lifestyles. Unfortunately, their lifestyles do not include growing national income fast enough to pay back the debt. So the Euro wobbled as investors tried to guess whether the EU would bail out Greece and, if so, whether that was good or bad. The three-week drop in the U.S. markets was the worst since the March 2009 bottom.

Greece is interesting because they have the same problems most of the Western world issuers of sovereign debt have, with two differences. They don't have their own currency, so they can't debase the euro to get out of their predicament. And they are small enough so the rest of Euroland doesn't have to knuckle under and bail the country out – although that may happen. (The Maastricht Treaty has a no-bailout clause, so it would be called something else.) So what happens to Greece will be a "tell" for what is going to happen in a lot of countries. Unless we get our fiscal and monetary houses in order – a real longshot – that includes the U.S.

Greece and the other PIIGS joined the euro currency zone with a promise to keep their annual government fiscal deficit under 3.0% of their Gross Domestic Product (GDP). These countries are all three to five times above their contracted level. Greece was at 13% last year, Spain at 11.4% and Portugal has a 9.2% deficit-to-GDP ratio. That has worried the credit markets enough to increase the PIIGS cost of credit relative to France or Germany by as much as one percentage point, so far. An extra percentage point on a debt load of 100% to 130% of GDP goes straight to the bottom line, increasing their deficit. That increases their credit spread further, which increases their deficit further, which increases their credit spread further...you get the picture.

Most of these countries have a long history of not being willing to tighten their belts, with any efforts in that direction thwarted by street demonstrations and a prompt voting out of office of whatever politician dared to suggest spending should be cut. Over 50% of their GDP is government spending, and they have one of the highest public employee levels as a percentage of population in Europe. Over half of their government budget is wages and pensions for public sector workers. A recent proposal to reduce these brought an immediate strike threat.

But Greece is in so deeply that they will either default, causing an immediate cessation of new credit and a very severe depression, or they have to be bailed out by France and Germany. France and Germany, already impacted by the worldwide recession, will not bail out Greece without strict requirements to cut spending and increase taxes. Increasing taxes is no problem, because Greeks don't pay taxes. Only six Greeks reported an income over $1 million in 2008. But cutting spending...well, there will be riots. Some politicians have said Germany has no right to ask Greece to cut spending until it makes reparations for the damage caused in

World War II. The Germans pointed out that they paid 115 million deutschmarks to Greece in 1960, back when the Dmark bought a lot of stuff, for that very purpose. But the grumbling continues.

Although the PIIGS account for about 40% of Eurozone GDP, Greece alone is only 2.3% of GDP. Its economy is about the same size as Michigan or Ohio. If it were Spain or Italy going under, there would not be much wiggle room. But with Greece the options are there:

1. Let them default on their debt and take the ensuing depression as best they can. Last year their GDP fell 3%. It is expected to drop 1.1% in 2010 and 0.3% in 2011, before any default. European banks hold a lot of Greek debt, but it would be cheaper to bail out the banks than bail out Greece.

2. Let them pull out of the euro and issue high-yield debt in drachmas to roll over their debt and continue to fund a lifestyle they cannot afford

3. Bail them out without serious conditions, thus destroying the world's faith in the euro as a strong currency

4. Bail them out with serious conditions, and let them deal politically with the riots

5. Bail them out with serious conditions, but don't enforce the conditions, so everyone can pretend that the euro is sound and the Greeks are trying to become fiscally responsible

As you have probably guessed, I think (5) is the most likely course of action. It follows the #1 rule of modern government, which is kick the can down the road so no one can blame the current incumbents. The euro would weaken against the dollar, but not disappear in a breakup of the Eurozone. It would not even have to be rejiggered, even though the Greeks and other

Southern Tier countries came in at an exchange rate that was set too high, creating an inflationary boom of consumer and government spending in the new additions to the Eurozone. And it lets the Greeks continue to live high on the hog, if not quite as high as before.

The Pain in Spain

Spain is a different story. It has an economy about the size of California running large deficits, and like California a default would have a significant impact on the larger union. France and Germany could simply guarantee Spain's debt, without actually sending them any money, conditional on Spain hitting various marks for reducing their deficit as a percent of GDP. This year they expect to be down to 4.6%, which is substantial progress. And their public-debt-to-GDP ratio is 60%, about half of Greece's ratio. Unlike Greece, Spain seems to eager to get their economy back in line, and both willing and able to suffer some short-term pain to get there. Recently, Spain tried to get the EC to agree to penalties for countries that don't hit their economic targets, and they were blocked by Germany. I think Spain can work their way out of their mess a lot easier than Greece or Italy.

The U.S. – The Next Greece?

Government spending in the U.S. has been on an unsustainable growth path for years, as shown in the graphic next page.

Government spending has grown seven times as much as median household income in real, inflation-adjusted dollars over the last 40 years, since Lyndon Johnson's "guns and butter" non-financing of the Vietnam War. The Reagan Revolution, Clinton budget "surplus" and 12 years of two Republican "small government" (in theory)

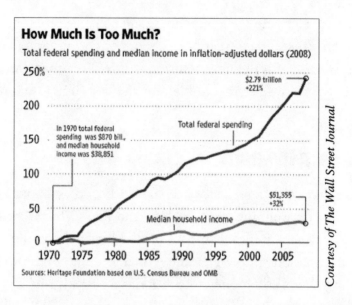

How Much Is Too Much?

Total federal spending and median income in inflation-adjusted dollars (2008)

$2.79 trillion
+221%

In 1970 total federal spending was $870 bill., and median household income was $38,851

Total federal spending

$51,355
+32%

Median household income

Sources: Heritage Foundation based on U.S. Census Bureau and OMB

Courtesy of The Wall Street Journal

Bushes notwithstanding, much of this spending creates constituencies that expect to continue to receive it in the future. More than half of all Americans now get more money from the government than they pay in taxes. With the best government money can buy and, Ron Paul and Alan Grayson excepted, not a statesman in sight, will the U.S. go the way of Greece?

If the Greeks could print euros, they would never become fiscally responsible. The U.S. can print dollars. I simply don't see the political will to take anything other than the easy way out, at least until other countries stop accepting dollars and dollar-denominated debt. With Euroland in work-out mode for the next decade, that means only China and Japan can impose fiscal responsibility on the U.S. The Japanese, who once again have become the largest holders of U.S. debt, probably are too polite to call us on the carpet. The Chinese, who have been trading Treasury debt for hard assets as quickly as is politically feasible, only care to protect the value of their dollar debt holdings. As soon as they can get rid of most of it, they could care less what happens to the U.S.

Sometime in the next three years, we are likely to see a dollar/euro crisis, as both currencies decline versus both real, internationally-traded assets like forest products, metals and food, and also harder currencies like the Canadian and Australian dollar. China will have to substantially weaken or break the link between the yuan and the U.S. dollar, or risk severe imported inflation.

I hope I'm wrong. I hope our government is more responsible and functional than Greece's government. I hope our unions and entitlement groups are more willing to take the pain than Greece's. I even hope our creditors are more forgiving than Greece's. But hope is not an investment strategy, and you need to prepare for the worst. The easiest way to make past debt irrelevant is to inflate one's currency. The Greeks have to leave the Eurozone to do it. The U.S. doesn't even have that constraint.

Hyperinflation

Hyperinflation in the U.S. is not the most likely outcome of the present monetary and fiscal policies, but I would put the odds of that outcome at somewhere around 30%. The most distressing factor of the whole financial crises is that the government has put the country in a position where hyperinflation even has to be considered.

One problem with hyperinflation is that governments always try to cope with it initially by imposing strict currency and asset flow controls. We have already seen the regulation on December 14, 2006 to limit the exportation and melting of penny and nickel coins. You may only take five dollars worth of these coins out of the country.

Under new regulations, if you are thinking of leaving the U.S. to live somewhere else until the storm blows over, the government will make you pay your estate tax in advance before you depart, and probably will tax you for 10 years after you depart, even if you never make another penny in the United States. If you try to move financial assets out of the country, you will find it harder to open a bank account due to reporting requirements imposed on overseas banks by President Obama's Hiring Incentives to Restore Employment (HIRE) Act, enacted March 18, 2010. You can still buy real estate or gold overseas and not report it, but that should be the next loophole to close.

If we endure only the Great Inflation, Social Security payments are supposed to rise with increases in the Consumer Price Index. But the keeper of the Consumer Price Index is the same government that has to pay the increases, and the temptation for them to revise the CPI lower is overwhelming. They have been doing this for years, substituting "owner's rent" for house prices when house prices were exploding, and making "hedonic adjustments" for things like personal computers. The desktop PC you bought five years ago cost $1,200. The one you just bought also cost $1,200, but because it runs four times as fast and has four times the storage, the CPI prices it as if it only cost $300 ($1,200 divided by 4). You probably couldn't find one that ran as slow as the one from five years before, so whether that one is now "worth" $300 is totally irrelevant to your cash flow today. You wanted a loaded desktop PC, so you paid the same $1200 you always have to pay. But it reduced the CPI.

John Williams at ShadowStats.com has tracked the CPI as if the Bureau of Labor Statistics had never changed it, compared to the as-reported number. I am not saying the "real" cost of living equals his unchanged number, just that the differences are quite large and some seems awfully arbitrary.

In 1970 I bought a nice suburban house in Mill Valley California for $30,000. By 2005 that house was valued at $500,000. It's certainly easy for people look back and say: "If only we'd held onto that house we bought 35 years ago, it would now be worth half a million."

But by 2030, which is a short 20 years away, that same house will probably sell for $30 million. Our grandkids will just shake their heads at the idea of buying a house like that for only $500,000. The Dow would be at 100,000, gold would be $10,000 an ounce, and silver would be $250 an ounce. And the $1,200 a month Social Security check the government promised you will buy 20 lattes at Starbucks.

If we go into hyperinflation, all those numbers become meaningless. Hyperinflation only happens in response to powerful deflationary forces that keep depressing tax revenues and creating "surprising" budget deficits. Governments print money to cover the deficits until creditors lose confidence in the currency, and the collapse in the value of the currency creates hyperinflation. The prices of everything get marked up to extreme levels not because they are more valuable, but because the currency they are being priced in is less and less valuable, until it is valueless. It doesn't matter if other countries are competitively devaluing at the time, which (for example) might make the U.S. dollar "strong" against the euro of British pound. If all three of those currencies are losing value in a Great Inflation or hyperinflation, your standard of living will be far more impacted by the value of the currency measured in real stuff, rather than relative to another losing currency.

Of course, if there is a currency that is not losing value – the Chinese yuan, perhaps – you would be much better off holding it.

Could Hyperinflation Ever Really Happen in America?

Easily. The U.S. government has spent the last couple of years trying to boost total demand levels, in an effort to substitute public demand for falling private demand. The government does that by running a gigantic fiscal deficit.

At the same time, the Fed has spent the last couple of years trying to boost total asset prices, in an effort to avoid an interest rate trap that would lead to a deflationary spiral. The Fed does that by "quantitative easing" – printing money.

Neither seems to understand that a big part of falling private demand is from demographics and generational economics. Nor do they pay any attention to the worldwide impact of accelerating technology change on falling prices, or how to transfer housing for a generation of 75.8 million people to a generation of 41.1 million people without lower prices.

So we can count on both the government and the Fed, hand-in-hand, to continue to run gigantic fiscal deficits and print money.

It is important to realize that *hyperinflation is not just a really bad inflation*. They have only one thing in common: Your dollars continue to lose purchasing power. But in the Great Inflation that is coming, they lose purchasing power because at some point there is so much money sloshing around that the economy really does pick up.

The demand for resources then accelerates rapidly, because the government and the Fed created far too much money in their attempt to get the economy moving. The government is incapable of cutting spending, so the fiscal deficit and fiscal stimulus will fall only slowly, as tax revenues pick up. Chairman Bernanke thinks he will be able to reverse his quantitative easing when the time comes, but he is certain to be late, as the Fed always is. He might not even be able to do much at all, depending on how loud the cries are for his head because he is "choking off the recovery" and "hurting Main Street."

Mix that with continued rapid growth in China, India, Brazil and other countries, and the ingredients for a classic, demand-driven inflation are obvious. I give that outcome a 70% probability of happening.

But hyperinflation is entirely different. Prices don't rise because the demand for goods and services is so high, or because unions can force through wage increases. Prices rise because people don't want to hold the currency. A hyperinflation can come directly out of a deflationary period like the one we have been in, without an intermediate stop at a sustainable expansion. It needs a spark to start it, but once a few people start getting rid of their currency as quickly as possible for gold, silver, canned goods, cars, ammunition, oil, acquiring companies, buying buildings or whatever they think they might need in the future, it can spiral out of control very quickly.

What might be the spark for a U.S. hyperinflation? Sadly, the worst Fed regime ever has created numerous possibilities. When a country has an annual deficit equal to 10% of GDP, and total debt equal to 100% of GDP, it is hard to show much real economic growth. So the Fed loans money to the banks at essentially no cost, and the banks buy newly-issued Treasury bonds and book the spread as income to rebuild their balance sheets. The Fed either buys toxic assets from the banks at 100 cents on the dollar, or changes the accounting rules so the banks can continue to carry the toxic assets at cost, without writing them down. That supports asset prices. At the same time, the Fed has made it possible for the banks to support the government's efforts to support aggregate demand.

The only problem is that the world is awash in Treasury paper that has been in a bull market for 28 years, pays the lowest interest rate ever, and cannot possibly be paid back. U.S. Treasury debt is a bigger bubble than the Internet and real estate booms combined.

So here's one way hyperinflation could start : Suppose the price of oil, a global commodity traded in dollars, jumps. It could be a misstep in the Middle East, or a realization that production is falling rapidly from many "elephant" oil fields, or OPEC moving from pricing in dollars to pricing in a basket of currencies, or something unforeseen, or nothing obvious at all. Maybe oil just starts to follow the price of gold.

Whatever the cause, hedge funds sell something to get the cash to jump on the oil trade. The easy thing to sell is Treasurys, reallocating assets from debt to commodities. Other managers follow. Not only is there selling pressure on Treasurys, but these investors will not show up at the next auction.

The auctions these days are large and frequent, and one of the biggest buyers is the British government. At least, that is what is reported. Since we know the new British government has no spare money and is operating under an austerity budget and cut-to-the-bone mentality, a lot of people on Wall Street think the real buyer, using the Brits as a front, is...Ben Bernanke. The Chinese and other buyers seem to have little impact these days, yet Bernanke cannot afford to have a "failed" Treasury auction. *A failed auction would be the spark for hyperinflation.*

So the Fed would step in and buy any bonds to make up for any institutional or foreign government shortfall in demand. The trouble is, everyone would see it, even if it was all done through a British front. With Treasury prices holding up and the oil play still attractive, even more asset managers would be encouraged to trim back their bonds and buy oil. The Fed is very sensitive to jiggles in the Treasury market, and would step in immediately to sop up this sudden supply. What would really be bad would be if the Too Big To Fail banks, who also would realize there is sudden selling pressure on Treasury bonds, saw an opportunity to get rid of part of their gross overallocation of Treasury bonds at a profit as long as the Fed is the buyer of last resort, propping up prices. At the very least, their traders would see a chance to sell bonds now and buy them back cheaper in the near future.

Now you have the rest of the market seeing that the only reason the last auction worked was that the Fed stepped in, and there was a lot of follow-on selling of bonds, even by the coddled Too Big To Fail banks, with the Fed the only buyer. Uh-oh. Their computers, if not their Investment Committees, will tell them to get the hell out.

These are the ingredients for a "flash crash" in the Treasury bond market. It just takes a moment to calculate that if Treasury bonds just go to market yields, the interest cost will put the U.S. deficit over $2 trillion very quickly, and that will make interest rates go even higher, and that will make the deficit go over $2.5 trillion very quickly, and...

All of a sudden it looks a lot smarter to buy commodities, hard assets and the necessities of day-to-day life before their prices shoot up or they disappear from store shelves. That's where hyperinflation begins. The whole process, from failed auction to empty store shelves, can take as little as a week. Gasoline can go from $3.50 a gallon to $10 a gallon in a week, and the stores will be out of gas cans for those trying to beat the next week's increase to $50 a gallon.

Hyperinflations are terrible. Those with a lot of debt that is not matched very carefully to assets that appreciate don't really win. Sure, their debt is wiped out. But they have to sell their assets to buy food, in competition with everyone else selling assets to buy food. Excluding jewelry and dental fillings, with metal content worth 5% to 10% of what you pay for them, less than 1% of Americans own any meaningful amount of gold. That silver dollar you got in your Christmas stocking when you were nine may buy a couple of days of food, but it is not going to make a meaningful difference.

I said in the introduction that in hyperinflation, society simply breaks down. That is the lesson of the Weimar Republic, Argentina and Zimbabwe. Wives have to prostitute themselves in return for a junk silver dime, or canned goods and stored grains, or watch their children die. The police and firefighters can't be paid, or can't buy anything with the dollars they are paid, and have to stop going to work in order to tend to their families. Neighborhoods band together to protect what they have, as gangs of starving people take things from others. Children work all day long collecting cardboard to burn for heat or trade for food. The unlucky will mix vegetable shortening with dirt and salt and make sun-dried dirt cookies just to stop the hunger pangs.

I realize this sounds ridiculous. But it has happened elsewhere, and I now give hyperinflation a 30% chance of happening here. And if it does, the Fed has a 0% chance of stopping it. Why? Because the Fed has acted by buying toxic assets, and paying with Treasury bonds or dollars. But what can they do if Treasury bonds *are* the toxic assets, and no one wants to hold dollars?

The answer is in Chapter 13, but the bad news for Chairman Bernanke is that it begins with taking all central bank functions away from the Fed.

The Austerity "Solution"

Lots of people, from European leaders to Tea Party members to most of Wall Street think the solution to our current problems is to embrace the deflation, cut government spending, balance the budget and let the chips fall where they may. The trouble with that course of action is that one of the first-order effects is a collapse in tax revenues, and instead of the budget deficit getting smaller, it gets larger. That requires a second round of spending cuts, which pushes the economy down further, resulting in another fall in tax revenues, a bigger instead of smaller budget deficit, another round of spending cuts...you get the picture. Because it doesn't "work" on the first round, but requires an extended depression with periodic government action to make the situation worse in the short run, it is politically impossible.

Also, it has been tried before. After the first leg down of the Great Depression, from 1929 to 1932, there was a period of stability and economic growth from 1932 to 1936. GDP grew at a 10% annual rate, bringing unemployment down from 25% in 1933 to 11% in 1937. The stock market compounded at 20% a year for the four years.

But for the election of 1936, President Roosevelt decided he needed to appear fiscally prudent. The government had been running deficits for six years, getting out of the first leg down. Republican critics were having a field day. So in the Democratic Party platform of 1936, Roosevelt said: "We hold this truth to be self-evident – that 12 years of Republican leadership left our Nation sorely stricken in body, mind, and spirit; and that three years of Democratic leadership have put it back on the road to restored health and prosperity...We have raised the public credit to a position of unsurpassed security. The interest rate on government bonds has been reduced to the lowest level in 28 years... We are determined to reduce the expenses of government... Our retrenchment, tax, and recovery programs thus reflect our firm determination to achieve a balanced budget and the reduction of the national debt at the earliest possible moment."

This prudent language helped him win reelection, but he forget the #1 Rule of Politics: Promise them anything before the election, and forget about it after the election. Roosevelt actually tried to balance the budget by a series of tax increases, while unemployment was still at 11%.

The results were entirely predictable. The second leg down of the Great Depression in 1937-1938 was brutal. Unemployment almost doubled from 11.2% in May 1937 to 20.0% in July 1938, as GDP fell by 5.4% in 1938. The stock market collapsed 49% from March 1937 to March 1938 and was still down 30% a year later. Four years of price recovery from the 1928-1932 deflation gave way to 3% annual deflation. With income, output and prices falling as unemployment shot up, Roosevelt never balanced the budget, although for one month in 1938 he got the deficit down to $89 billion.

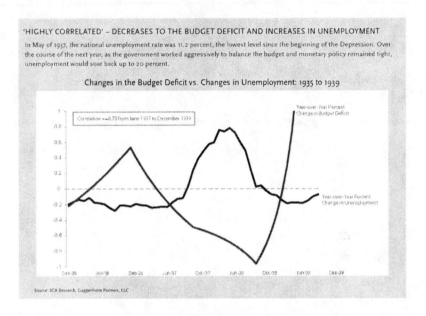

'HIGHLY CORRELATED' – DECREASES TO THE BUDGET DEFICIT AND INCREASES IN UNEMPLOYMENT

In May of 1937, the national unemployment rate was 11.2 percent, the lowest level since the beginning of the Depression. Over the course of the next year, as the government worked aggressively to balance the budget and monetary policy remained tight, unemployment would soar back up to 20 percent.

Changes in the Budget Deficit vs. Changes in Unemployment: 1935 to 1939

That was a gentler time. If President Obama and Chairman Bernanke try to withdraw the stimulus while unemployment is anywhere near current levels, there will be rioting in the streets of America, just as there was in Greece. With a Fed Chairman who is acutely conscious of the consequences of President Roosevelt's change in policies in 1936, there is not a chance it will happen here.

CHAPTER 7

Exactly How Can The Fed Do This?

(OR, THE FED IN A NUTSHELL, WHERE THEY BELONG)

Remember that credit is money.

—Benjamin Franklin

his is the 100-year anniversary of the 1910 secret meeting at Jekyll Island, Georgia, that resulted in the founding of the Federal Reserve Bank in 1913. There have been a lot of accurate, interesting histories written about the Fed, including *Secrets of the Temple: How the Federal Reserve Runs the Country* by William Greider, and *The Creature from Jekyll Island: A Second Look at the Federal Reserve* by G. Edward Griffin. For a more extreme viewpoint, Murray Rothbard's *The Case Against The Fed* is the classic text. I won't try to repeat all that history, but just summarize the key points.

The seven men who met at the Jekyll Island Club represented about 25% of the private wealth of America at the time. The point of the meeting was to work out the ground rules for a new central back – the U.S. had already had two or three central banks that failed. The key decision was that the Central Bank would not be a U.S. government agency, but would be collectively owned by the various banks in the U.S.

At the time, of course, the U.S. dollar was backed by gold. If the government ran a deficit, it had to sell gold to get the cash to meet its bills, or print money now and then buy gold to back it later. With a Central Bank, it would be easier to borrow money to be repaid later out of tax receipts. But instead of issuing Treasury Notes – dollars – to cover deficits, the Federal Reserve would issue Federal Reserve Notes. Where the government did not owe any interest on a Treasury Note, it would have to pay interest on any Federal Reserve Notes (cash) that it borrowed. After President Franklin Roosevelt took us off the gold standard in 1933, it was clear that the only difference between the Treasury printing money and the Fed creating credit was that the government had to pay interest on Fed credit. That is why the additional debt being piled up today is especially pernicious; we and our children will have to pay interest on it for years, and like buying a car or a house with credit, it could cost two or three times its face value over the repayment period.

In addition to providing credit to the Federal government, the Fed is charged with regulating its bank members, setting the short-term reference rate at which banks borrow from the Fed and therefore from each other, controlling the supply of money, and maintaining a stable value of the dollar. Since 1913, the dollar has lost about 95% of its value to inflation, so I think we can write that last mandate off as a total failure. It became obvious in 2007-2008 that they don't do a great job of regulating their members, either, except in the driest accounting sense. That leaves setting short term interest rates as their biggest public impact, and controlling the money supply as their biggest private impact.

Changes in short-term rates, the *price* of money, make headlines. Changes in the money supply, the *quantity* of money, don't. I'm not sure why that is, but I think the Fed itself has made it deliberately easy for reporters and the public to understand the interest rate, and somewhat obscure to understand the quantity. I remember some years ago getting a call from a Congressman's office. He was going to grill Fed Chairman Greenspan at a hearing, and he wanted to know how the Fed controls the money supply. When I explained that they simply bought Treasury bonds from banks to pump money into the economy, and sold T-bonds to banks when they wanted to sop the money back up, he was astonished. He actually asked me what the Fed would do it the banks refused to buy the T-bonds when the Fed wanted to sell. I explained to him that when the Fed says jump, the *only* acceptable answer is: "How high?"

It is very convenient for the Fed that the media and the public are focused on the Fed funds rate. The Fed can keep that rate low, as they are now, while quietly tightening the money supply. Or they can move the rate up at the end of a boom to show they are policing the situation, while still printing money and creating credit to fund the most recent asset bubble. Of course, Chairman Bernanke just came right out and said he has a program of "quantitative easing." People heard that phrase and their eyes glazed over. If he had said "printing money" there might have been more resistance.

One of the very silly things the deflationists are saying right now is that first we will have a terrible deflation, and then the U.S. will turn on the printing presses and destroy the dollar. They never explain why Ben Bernanke, an avowed enemy of deflation and an expert on the Great Depression, wouldn't turn on the printing presses to avoid the deflation in the first place. *He is already doing just that.* Deflation increases the real debt burden of the three most profligate entities in our society: consumers, the Federal government and the state governments. Inflation decreases the real debt burden. There is no reason in the world for Bernanke to not choose inflation, except that it will continue to lower the value of the dollar. Since the Fed has been lowering the value of the dollar for 97 years, I doubt they will change course now.

Another silly thing the deflationists say is that Bernanke can't print money fast enough to avoid deflation, due to the magnitude of the wealth destruction in stocks and real estate. Bernanke does not literally have to print a single dollar. An electronic deposit to one or many banks is all it takes to create money. If President Obama implemented a $1 trillion stimulus package tomorrow, the Fed could fund it in 30 seconds if they had to.

What's wrong with this picture? Pretty much everything. The central bank should be owned by the government, and any money it creates for deficit financing should not accrue interest. Instead of 12 Federal Reserve members setting monetary policy as if they actually knew what they were doing and had an accurate crystal ball, the money supply should grow by a very modest percentage every year – 2% or less – and let the market sort it out. The Federal government needs to balance its budget as soon as possible, but not by raising the income tax or drastically cutting spending. They should replace all personal and corporate income taxes with a sales tax that is refundable at the border for exports. About a 22% sales tax on everything but rent and unprocessed food, combined with a monthly grant for the poorest, would keep the tax burden off the poor. Making the sales tax refundable at the border would help our manufacturing and service companies compete in global markets with the only legal subsidy left. Our trading partners are refunding VAT for exports; why can't we refund a sales tax?

This policy change would get the economy growing, which would increase revenues from the 22% tax. At the same time, the elimination of all income taxes gets rid of a huge bureaucratic burden on individuals and corporations, and makes the U.S. a magnet for fresh capital.

Perhaps best of all, it focuses the Fed on the job they are supposed to do but don't: Regulate the banking system so we don't get into another mess like 1979 (oil), 1982 (South America), 1986 (S&Ls), 2000 (Y2K) and 2007 (real estate). And by taking away their central bank functions, it demotes the Fed to the level where they should have been at all along, both Constitutionally and based on their sorry record to date.

CHAPTER 8

What Is The Fed Doing
(AND HOW TO TRACK IT)

The king's cheese is half wasted in parings;
but no matter, 'tis made of the people's milk.
—Benjamin Franklin

The Fed operates quietly, but the numbers are not hard to find. You can track the path to inflation and verify that I am right with only three sources: The St. Louis Fed, John Williams' ShadowStats.com, and the Fed itself. Here's what you want to watch – and it won't cost you anything (although I encourage anyone who can afford to support John Williams to subscribe).

The Federal Reserve Bank of St. Louis

The St. Louis Fed has always been the most monetarist of the regional Federal Reserve Banks, and has been faithfully chronicling the money supply, inflation, interest rates and almost everything else you need to know ever since I've been in the investment business. You can find their full list of publications at http://www. stlouisfed.org/publications/show_all.cfm. The only two you need to

follow are the weekly *U.S. Financial Data* found at http://research.
stlouisfed.org/publications/usfd/ and the monthly *Monetary Trends*
found at http://research.stlouisfed.org/publications/mt/.

U.S. Financial Data

Right under the current date on the *U.S. Financial Data* home
page, you will find a link for "Entire Publication (Final Edition)."
This is a .pdf file that requires a .pdf reader like Adobe Acrobat to
open, available free from http://www.adobe.com. The publication
includes weekly updates for:

- Page 3 — Adjusted Monetary Base
- Page 4 — Adjusted Reserves
- Page 5 — MZM
- Page 6 — M2
- Page 7 — Composition of Federal Reserve Assets and
  Liabilities
- Page 8 — Reserve Bank Credit and Selected Categories
- Page 9 — Other Federal Reserve Balance Sheet Items
- Page 10 — Yields on Selected Securities
- Page 11 — Corporate Bond Spreads and Mortgage Interest
  Rates
- Page 12 — Yields on Nominal and Inflation-Indexed
  Treasury Securities
- Page 13 — Federal Funds Futures Market
- Page 14 — Equity Price Indices
- Page 15 — Crude Oil Prices
- Page 16 — Natural Gas Prices
- Page 17 — Exchange Rates
- Page 18 — Currency, Savings, and Small Time Deposits
- Page 19 — Institutional and Retail Money Funds, and
  Borrowings from Federal Reserve Banks

- Page 20 — Bank Loans
- Page 21 — Commercial Paper Outstanding
- Page 22 — Reference Tables

Each page can be downloaded separately, and the ones you will care about most are pages 3, 5 and 6, which measure the monetary aggregates that are more-or-less ignored by Keynesian economists. The others are very useful from time to time; for example, to track whether banks are actually making loans.

The **Adjusted Monetary Base** on page 3 is defined as what households and businesses use as media of exchange, and that depository institutions use to satisfy statutory reserve requirements and to settle interbank debts. This includes currency (including coin) held outside the Treasury and the Federal Reserve Banks (referred to as *currency in circulation*) plus deposits held by depository institutions at the Federal Reserve Banks. The demand by the private sector for these forms of money is what gives the Federal Reserve leverage to affect money market interest rates.

Although most of the other Federal Reserve Banks and the Fed in Washington pay little attention to the monetary base, I focus on the long-run implications of monetary base growth for the price level and inflation rate. Milton Friedman famously said: "Inflation is always and everywhere a monetary phenomenon." In the long run, the inflation rate is determined by the growth rate of money because without such growth, inflation could not continue. So it doesn't matter whether policymakers are targeting interest rates, as they are today, or monetary aggregates, as they used to target and will again. As long as their actions *permit* the necessary increases in the central bank's balance sheet, inflation will follow.

Skipping ahead to page 6, **M2** is the most-watched measure of the amount of money in the economy. M1 is physical money, all the currency and coins in circulation, plus checking accounts. It is a measure of the most liquid part of the money supply. M2 is M1 plus savings accounts, bank CDs and retail or individual money market mutual funds. These are all just slightly less liquid than cash and checks.

M3 is, or was, M2 plus all large CDs, institutional money-market funds, short-term repurchase agreements and some other large liquid assets. The Fed suddenly decided that it cost too much money to calculate M3 and it wasn't a very useful number, so they discontinued publishing it on March 13, 2006. One guy with a personal computer now calculates it (so much for cost) and provides it to a large number of subscribers (so much for usefulness). It probably will not surprise you that shortly after the Fed discontinued calculating the series, M3 shot up in the early days of the 2007-2008 downturn.

Money Zero Maturity (MZM) on page 5 is M2 *minus* small-denomination time deposits and *plus* all money market funds. It is calculated by the St. Louis Fed. They are trying to track the amount of money readily available for current spending and consumption transactions.

Searching on the St. Louis Fed's website for individual pages will give you a long-term graph like this one on M2 from 1981 to the present:

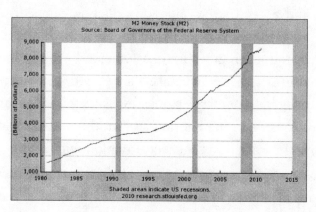

The weekly *U.S. Financial Data* page 6 for M2 covers a shorter period, about 14 months, in more detail:

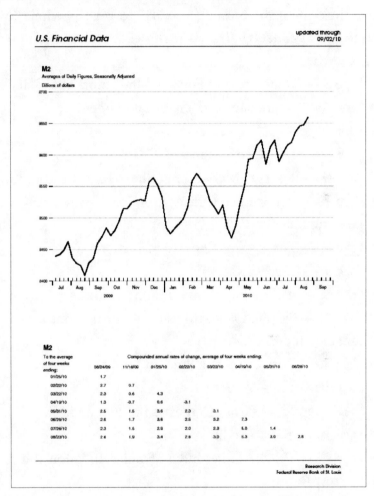

The very useful part of this you might not immediately recognize is the triangle at the bottom. Publication dates run both up and down and left to right. The numbers in the table are the annualized growth rate between any two dates. You can watch money supply growth rates rise and fall on this chart, and see if the Fed is changing direction or running very loose or very tight. The St. Louis Fed puts a table like this at the bottom of each page in *U.S. Financial Data*.

Monetary Trends

As with *U.S. Financial Data*, you can get the individual pages or just click "Published Issue (8.5x11)" to get the whole thing. The monthly *Monetary Trends* includes a major essay on the cover, and then:

- Page 3 — Monetary and Financial Indicators at a Glance
- Monetary Aggregates and Their Components
    - Page 4 — Aggregates
    - Page 5 — Components
- Page 6 — Reserves Markets and Short-Term Credit Flows
- Page 7 — Senior Loan Officer Opinion Survey on Bank Lending Practices
- Page 8 — Measures of Expected Inflation
- Page 9 — Interest Rates
- Page 10 — Policy-Based Inflation Indicators
- Page 11 — Implied Forward Rates, Futures Contracts, and Inflation-Indexed Securities
- Velocity, Gross Domestic Product, and M2
    - Page 12 — Velocity
    - Page 13 — Gross Domestic Product and M2
- Page 14 — Bank Credit
- Page 15 — Stock Market Index, Foreign Inflation and Interest Rates
- Reference Tables
    - Page 16 — Monetary Data
    - Page 17 — Interest Rates
    - Page 18 — Monetary Aggregate Growth Rates

Page 4 shows the aggregate indices M1, M2 and MZM one above the other, but I like page 5, which shows the components of the indices. It looks like this:

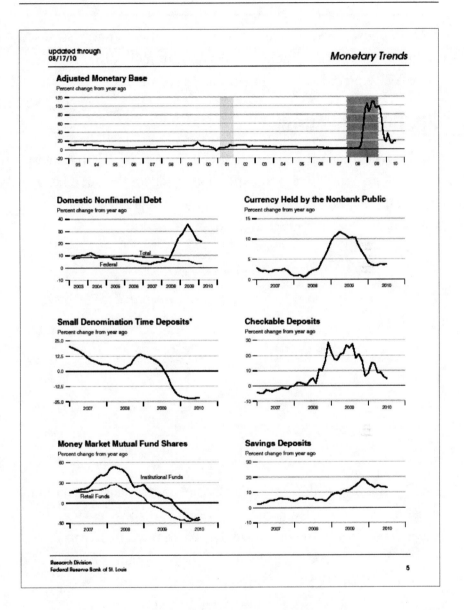

You also will want to look at page 8 – Measures of Expected Inflation, page 10 – Policy-Based Inflation Indicators, and page 12 – Velocity. Page 12 is especially important right now, as the Fed's efforts to simulate the economy by shoveling money into the banks are being thwarted by the banks sitting on it, not loaning it out, and simply reinvesting it in Treasury securities. That has caused Velocity to fall, and economic activity equals money times velocity. As velocity picks back up, inflationary pressures rise.

ShadowStats.com

John Williams of ShadowStats.com continued calculating M3 after the Fed said it was too expensive to collect the data. He also calculates the Consumer Price Index as if various changes since the Reagan Administration had not been made.

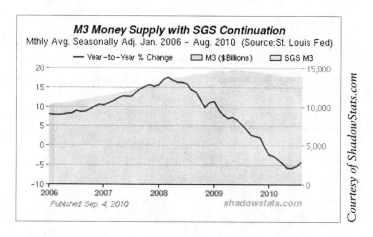

The dramatic fall in M-3 reflects a collapse in short-term repurchase agreements as banks at first refused to do business with each other due to fear of the unknown damage in the counterparty's real estate exposure, and then due to the huge amount of nearly free money from the Fed that flowed onto their balance sheets.

The Bureau of Labor Statistics has steadily changed the Consumer Price Index to "improve" it, with the result that the annual adjustment in Social Security payments, union contracts and numerous other costs and incomes has been much lower than it would have been. For example, the Social Security adjustment for 2010 was zero, based on the red lower line on the ShadowStats.

com graphic repeated below. It should have been about 6% based on the blue upper line.

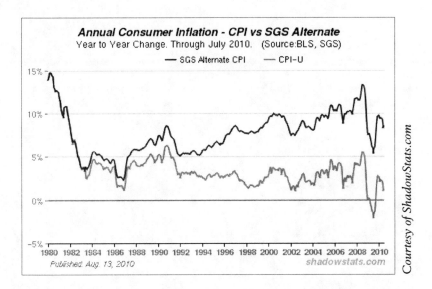

Courtesy of ShadowStats.com

This becomes important in making decisions about how to protect yourself against inflation or hyperinflation. Treasury Inflation-Protected Securities (TIPS) are inflation-indexed bonds offered in 5-, 10- and 30-year maturities, where the principal is adjusted by changes in the Consumer Price Index. They now account for about 8% of all Treasury debt. In an accelerating inflation, it is likely that more and more individuals and institutions would buy them. It therefore becomes more and more attractive for the government to continue to "improve" the Consumer Price Index calculation in a way that shows smaller increases in the CPI.

John Templeton Warns from Beyond the Grave

'Tis easy to see, hard to foresee.
—Benjamin Franklin

I was a guest at the Lyford Cay Club in the Bahamas and met Sir John Templeton in 1993 at the funeral of his second wife, Irene. He was 80 then, and very much interested in the new technology and biotech stocks I was following. We talked at his beautiful home for a while, and I realized that my enthusiasm for the changes technology could bring fit right into the inherent optimism he had, which had served him so well in investing over the years. He was not afraid to wade into an area of confusion or a depressed market, because he believed people were better than they knew and would work it out. On the other hand, he was sharp enough to tell when things were overbought, and he would exit a market as if he were the Cheshire Cat. The last thing anyone would see was the smile, as he sold his last shares.

Sir John died on July 8, 2008, of pneumonia, at the age of 95 – still going strong, still curious and, I thought, still the optimist.

But it turns out that in June, 2005, he wrote a memo to his family and friends expressing his worries about what he saw coming for the U.S. and global economies. The memo was locked in a file of his personal papers, and only recently came to light. He wanted it shared widely, so I am doing my part. Here it is, unaltered.

John M. Templeton
Lyford Cay, Nassau, Bahamas
June 15, 2005

MEMORANDUM

Financial Chaos – probably in many nations in the next five years. The word chaos is chosen to express likelihood of reduced profit margin at the same time as acceleration in cost of living.

Increasingly often, people ask my opinion on what is likely to happen financially. I am now thinking that the dangers are more numerous and larger than ever before in my lifetime. Quite likely, in the early months of 2005, the peak of prosperity is behind us.

In the past century, protection could be obtained by keeping your net worth in cash or government bonds. Now, the surplus capacities are so great that most currencies and bonds are likely to continue losing their purchasing power.

Mortgages and other forms of debts are over tenfold greater now than ever before 1970, which can cause manifold increases in bankruptcy auctions.

Surplus capacity, which leads to intense competition, has already shown devastating effects on companies who operate airlines and is now beginning to show in companies in ocean shipping and other activities. Also, *the present surpluses of cash and liquid assets have pushed yields on bonds and mortgages almost to zero when adjusted for higher cost of living. Clearly, major corrections are likely in the next few years.*

Most of the methods of universities and other schools which require residence have become hopelessly obsolete. Probably over half of the universities in the world will disappear quickly over the next thirty years.

Obsolescence is likely to have a devastating effect in a wide variety of human activities, especially in those where advancement is hindered by labor unions or other bureaucracies or by government regulations.

Increasing freedom of competition is likely to cause most established institutions to disappear with the next fifty years, especially in nations where there are limits on free competition.

Accelerating competition is likely to cause profit margins to continue to decrease and even become negative in various industries. *Over tenfold more persons hopelessly indebted leads to multiplying bankruptcies not only for them but for many businesses that extend credit without collateral. Voters are likely to enact rescue subsidies, which transfer the debts to governments, such as Fannie May and Freddie Mac.*

Research and discoveries and efficiency are likely to continue to accelerate. Probably, as quickly as fifty years, as much as ninety percent of education will be done by electronics.

Now, with almost one hundred independent nations on earth and rapid advancements in communication, the top one percent of people are likely to progress more rapidly than the others. Such top one percent may consist of those who are multi-millionaires and also, those who are innovators and also, those with top intellectual abilities. *Comparisons show that prosperity flows toward those nations having most freedom of competition.*

Especially, electronic computers are likely to become helpful in all human activities including even persons who have not yet learned to read.

Hopefully, many of you can help us to find published journals and websites and electronic search engines to help us benefit from accelerating research and discoveries.

Not yet have I found any better method to prosper during the future financial chaos, which is likely to last many years, than to keep your net worth in shares of those corporations that have proven to have the widest profit margins and the most rapidly increasing profits. Earning power is likely to continue to be valuable, especially if diversified among many nations.

PART IV

What You Must Do – *Now*

Energy and persistence conquer all things.
—Benjamin Franklin

CHAPTER 9

Who Gets Hurt?

I conceive that the great part of the miseries
of mankind are brought upon them by false estimates
they have made of the value of things.

—Benjamin Franklin

The list of who gets hurt in the Great Inflation is long. Sadly, it is biased towards those who can least afford to get hurt: The retired and the poor. It also hurts the fiscally prudent who have spurned excessive credit and focused on saving money. And it hurts the conservative investor who own bonds, as well as the foreign countries who have bootstrapped themselves by manufacturing for the U.S. market, and now hold huge amounts of our debt.

The Great Inflation will push the value of the dollar down, push interest rates up, and push prices up. The right way to look at this is that it is the falling dollar that pushes prices up, as markets reprice everything to account for the fact that the dollar is less valuable. It also is the falling dollar that pushes interest rates up, as lenders try to earn enough extra annual interest to offset their annual loss in purchasing power. It all starts with the dollar.

The U.S. dollar is a loser against commodities in an inflation, by definition. Note that it does not have to go down against other currencies – they can all tank together. But it does seem likely that in a rip-roaring inflation, the currencies of resource-heavy countries like Canada and Australia should do better, unless their governments do something to screw them up.

As for all the others – well, no one knows if the euro can even survive the European Union's collective death wish to cut government spending in a recession. As for the Chinese yuan, in a high inflation their materials costs skyrocket, so the question is how fast they can raise their prices. Raising prices is what inflation is all about, but they have a long supply chain to get their goods to market, and Wal-Mart is not likely to go to cost-plus pricing. The Japanese yen has similar problems, although in lesser magnitude.

So the very first people hurt are those who hold dollars. That means U.S. corporations with lots of cash, which is at record levels. It means individuals building cash in the bank for peace of mind or because they believe a *de*flation is coming. And, very important, it means foreign holders of dollars and dollar-denominated debt, like Treasury notes and bills.

At this writing, about 40% of U.S. Government debt is held by public entities. The largest 15 holders at the end of May 2010 were:

1. Federal Reserve & Intergovernmental Holdings, $5.259 billion

2. Other Investors & Savings Bonds (individuals, government-sponsored enterprises, broker/dealers, bank personal trusts, estates, savings bonds, corporate and non-corporate businesses), $1.193 trillion

3. China, $900.2 billion, rising every month

4. Japan, $795.5 billion and flat

5. U.S. Mutual Funds (money market, open-end, closed-end), $663.9 billion, down $105 billion from December 2008, but still mostly held for U.S. individuals

6. State and Local Governments, $531.3 billion, about flat for three years

7. U. S. Pension Funds (private, local, state, Federal Employees Retirement System Thrift Savings Plan G Fund), $513.1 billion

8. United Kingdom, $321.2 billion, an all-time high up from $55 billion in June 2008. There is a possibility that much of this is actually held by the UK government on behalf of the Federal Reserve, and Chairman Bernanke tells them to show up at selected Treasury auctions to give the illusion of strong buying interest

9. Oil Exporters (Ecuador, Venezuela, Indonesia, Bahrain, Iran, Iraq, Kuwait, Oman, Qatar, Saudi Arabia, United Arab Emirates, Algeria, Gabon, Libya, Nigeria), $239.3 billion, just above their usual $190 billion to $220 billion range

10. Insurance Companies (property-casualty and life insurance), $235.7 billion

11. U.S. Depository Institutions (commercial banks, savings banks, credit unions), $206.6 billion, almost double the December 2008 level

12. Brazil, $164.3 billion, about flat for the last two years

13. Caribbean Banking Centers (Bahamas, Bermuda, Cayman Islands, Netherlands Antilles, Panama, British Virgin Islands), $153.2 billion, up from $106.6 billion in June 2008, but below the high of $213.6 billion in March 2009

14. Hong Kong, $151.8 billion, up 88% in one year

15. Taiwan, $126.9 billion, up 60% in one year to leapfrog Russia, which was selling U.S. debt and got their exposure down to $113.1 billion.

It may surprise you that the Federal Reserve System of banks is one of the top holders of Treasury debt. Before the Fed was created, if annual Federal government revenues from tariffs and taxes did not cover spending, the Treasury could print money and put it into circulation.

But after the government gave the Fed the power to create money, Treasury now sells a bond to the Fed to get the money to cover the shortfall. That means the taxpayer now has to pay annual interest on the money that is needed, instead of just letting Treasury print the money directly.

Needless to say, the Federal Reserve System was designed by bankers, who have profited mightily from it for the last 97 years at the expense of taxpayers. I think they will find a way to avoid being the most-harmed institution in the Great Inflation.

After the Fed, it is U.S. individuals that will feel the pain, either directly or through their trusts and estates, or #5 Mutual Funds. Savers and retired people tend to own Treasury debt, so the prudent and those who cannot recover from a dramatic decline in real incomes will be the losers.

After that we have China and Japan, the two biggest foreign owners of U.S. debt. Add in #9 Oil Exporters, #12 Brazil, #14 Hong Kong, #15 Taiwan and the Russians, and there is $2.5 trillion in U.S. debt owned by foreign governments.

We have four choices to deal with it:

1. Work long and hard to divert a big chunk of our GDP to pay it back (after we get our net new monthly borrowing down to zero, of course – an outcome that does not seem likely in the visible future)

2. Sell them large chunks of America – buildings, land, mining and petroleum assets, major companies
3. Inflate the burden away
4. Default

Hard work or selling assets is never popular with the voters, and formal default is both embarrassing and unnecessary. Chairman Bernanke will simply inflate the burden away, all the while saying a strong dollar policy is in America's best interest. Fed Chairmen have been saying that for the entire first 96% decline in the value of the dollar, and they will say it until the remaining 4% is gone.

In addition to the direct effects of a falling dollar on the real value of an investment, the inflation that is imported by steadily increasing prices for international commodities like paper and oil is diffused through the whole system. Pensioners still get the same amount of dollars every month, but the dollars don't go as far. The same is true of Social Security recipients, where payments lag inflation at best, or due to a manipulated CPI calculation, never catch up.

Landlords who have granted long-term leases find themselves squeezed by flat income in an inflationary world. On the flip side of that coin, tenants living month-to-month can expect regular, large increases in their rent. People on SSI disability or Section 8 rental assistance will get squeezed both ways, as landlords raise rents but their incomes lag inflation or don't increase at all.

Homeowners with adjustable rate mortgages will be shocked by the size and frequency of the adjustments, and many will join the ranks of the foreclosed upon or strategic defaulters.

In early 2010, driving very slowly in a Colorado snowstorm, I hit a patch of ice. In spite of all-wheel drive, the car slid to the side of the road. Colorado roads are bordered by deep ditches for water runoff, and I slid into the icy ditch and along until the right front fender hit a big cottonwood tree. The air bag didn't even deploy, I was going so slowly. But at the end of the day there was $23,000 worth of damage to the car.

The U.S. housing market is in the midst of a slow-motion wreck, and you need to know what you can do as an unwilling passenger when it hits the tree. In this case, the equivalent of the patch of ice that started me towards the tree is the number of adjustable-rate mortgages resetting, starting now. While everyone has worried about unemployment and negative equity keeping foreclosures high, the volume of ARM resets is likely to be at least as big a problem. Between 2010 and 2012, over $250 billion in option ARMs will reset. On most of these, the borrower has not been making payments that even covered the interest. Even with today's low interest rates, their monthly payments will skyrocket. About 75% of all option ARMs were written in California, Florida, Nevada and Arizona, and over 45% already are more than 30-days late, even though rates have reset on only about 12% of them.

Another $160+ billion in Alt-A loans will reset during those three years. These are the low-to-no documentation loans, also known as "liar loans," where the borrowers' ability to pay is completely unknown. Another $600 billion in standard ARMs will reset, meaning over $1 trillion in resets of ARM mortgages of varying quality will hit the banking system over the these three years. Many of these ARM mortgages cannot be refinanced into fixed-rate mortgages because either borrowers' credit scores have fallen or property values have fallen so far, so as interest rate increase they eventually will fall into foreclosure. Fed Chairman Bernanke will do what he knows how to do: Buy toxic assets from the lenders so they don't have to write them off, pump more money and credit into the system to prevent as many foreclosures as they can, and keep interest rates as low as possible. Bernanke has one simple cure for deflation: *Inflate!*

Another group that will be damaged by high inflation and a steady erosion in the dollar are the countries that link their currencies to the dollar, either formally or informally. Other countries besides the U.S. that use the U.S. dollar as their exclusive or an official currency are the British Virgin Islands, Ecuador, El Salvador, East Timor, Marshall Islands, Micronesia, Palau, Panama, Turks & Caicos Islands.

Hong Kong and China informally link to the dollar by taking market action to prevent the Hong Kong dollar or yuan to increase much, if any, against the U.S. dollar. This has been very useful to them in the past, but rapid inflation in the U.S. probably will force the informal links to break. The alternative would be to allow the prices of almost all their raw materials to skyrocket, and now that they are the factory floor to the world, they can't afford to let that happen.

China: Bull or Bear?

At *New World Investor* we got out of China at a fortuitous time in early 2008. I keep finding interesting businesses in China with relatively cheap stocks, especially in areas like gold and silver mining, medical devices and healthcare, and technology. But then I look at the overall situation, and I'm hesitant to pull the trigger. My friends Robert Hsu at *China Strategy* and Keith Fitz-Gerald at *Money Morning* are very bullish on China. But others I have broken bread with, like Jim Rogers, Marc Faber and Jim Chanos, are negative in varying degrees, especially on the near-term outlook for what could be a huge bubble in residential and commercial property. Jim Rogers moved his family to China because he believes it will be the dominant country of the 21ˢᵗ Century, and Marc lived in Hong Kong for years before moving to Thailand. They have a lot of skin in the game, and I take all five of these investors very seriously. So I think it is worth it to go through the facts and their analysis, and come to our own conclusions.

It is tempting to simply say that China is in a real estate bubble that will pop, just because it already happened in the U.S. and Europe. We know that real estate is so big that if it pops, it can bring down a whole economy. Maybe even enough to derail China's surge to become the leading economic power.

Bull?

But China also has a lot more momentum than the U.S. or Europe had going into their real estate problems. They are a creditor nation with a large trade surplus and rapid GDP growth, and have stockpiled $2.4 trillion of foreign reserves and 1,054 tonnes of gold. Taxes are low, regulations are lighter than in the U.S. or Europe, and more people are making lots more money or even getting rich than in either the U.S. or Europe. The Communist Party is simply an alternative career path where you get rich by skimming, and everyone understands that economic freedom is not political freedom to criticize the skimming or the Party. Think of the Party as the IRS of China.

With all these people making money, it is important to understand that there is no state welfare system in China. There are state-owned businesses where you can get a job and never get fired, but you still have to fund your own health care and retirement. Consequently, the Chinese have a very high savings rate, and they are all very interested in watching their savings grow. They're also very interested in education and self-improvement, for both themselves and their children. So, again, they pay informed attention to how their savings are doing, and where they should be redeployed.

Even though many more Chinese college students than Americans study the hard sciences like math and physics, including graduate study in the U.S., wages are low across the board. That is changing, and some very basic manufacturing processes are now being outsourced from China to Vietnam, Thailand or Myanmar. But the wage gap between China and Europe or the U.S. is so large that it will take decades to close. So they will have their labor -cost advantage as far as the eye can see.

The country also spends a fraction of what the U.S. and Europe do on defense. In spite of projecting military power with a few heavily-press released rocket launches, and having a big army in numbers (but small in percentage of population), China is not involved in any wars or military operations. Even during the Vietnam War, they lent aid and comfort and some rifles and bullets to Hanoi – but that was it. China's military budget is about $75 billion a year, and they don't have any foreign bases. The U.S. spends over $1 trillion a year on the military, with bases all over the world.

Bear?

First, China counts their GDP by what is produced, not by what is sold. So their numbers are at least different, and many would say the books are cooked. I look at their trade balance, though, and think that even if the numbers are somewhat high, they are still growing very rapidly for a country of their size.

Second, the banks are in thrall to the government, and when the government says "lend," the banks do it. By 1995, most of the state-owned banks were bankrupt on an honest mark-to-market, and it took years to work them out of their hole. Then the 2007 slowdown hit, and the targeted Chinese stimulus program required the banks to lend. Lend they did. And much of it was for real estate development – office buildings, new shopping malls, and entire new cities.

At the same time, while many Chinese buy and wear gold and enjoy gambling in the stock market, they buy real estate for retirement. It is not unusual for someone living in an apartment to buy two or three more apartments, even if they sit vacant, as a store of value to cash in someday. One recent government rules change temporarily blocks banks from giving a mortgage for a third apartment, while limiting loans on the first apartment to 80% and on the second to 60%. But only some of the buyers were using mortgages; many just pay cash.

So today there is a glut of high-end residential construction, as developers gamble on everyone continuing to get rich. And some apartments are still selling, even though (or maybe because) prices were up 50% in 2009 alone. But with apartment prices up to 15x average income, this is starting to look like Las Vegas housing at the height of the flipper frenzy. We know how that turned out.

The truly bad news is that the office building and commercial retail markets look even worse. The official office building vacancy rate today is 20%. Jim Chanos figured out that if all the current office buildings are completed, 30 billion ft^2 of space, there will be room for a 5'x5' cubicle for every person in China. And the poster child for retail construction disasters is the South China Mall, outside Dongguan, 40 miles from Guangzhou. It's the largest mall in the world, twice the size of the Mall of America, with 1,500 shops. All but four are empty and have been since the mall opened in 2005. It was financed almost entirely by bank credit, which can't be repaid, so the government stepped in to carry the loan. The annual maintenance cost must be enormous.

So the bear case is that easy money – Chinese M1 was up 35% in 2009 – has created a massive property bubble that is sure to pop. I think that's obvious. What is less obvious is what the government will do about it. The three largest banks in the world right now are Chinese, just as the world's largest banks at the peak of the Japanese property bubble were Japanese. I think they will tell the banks to *not* write off the bad loans immediately, but follow the U.S. Federal Reserve's "extend and pretend" accounting to slowly write these disasters off against earnings over time. If Bernanke can buy toxic assets from the banks at 100% of stated value, why can't the Chinese government do the same thing? Outsiders may never see the real numbers, because "transparency" is not considered a virtue or intelligent strategy in China. The banks will be bankrupt for a while, and then work it out without ever going through a formal reorganization. Many of these buildings will end up torn down, but some will survive to become useful infrastructure.

It is important to realize that China's real estate bubble is not about to collapse. It *is* collapsing. Just as Chairman Bernanke's famous March 2007 dictum that "the impact on the broader economy and financial markets of the problems in the subprime markets seems likely to be contained" lulled people to sleep for another year, the major China watchers are saying: "No problem."

Well, there is a problem. Apartment prices in major cities like Beijing have spiraled up to over 20x annual income. In Beijing, a 968 ft² apartment costs $236,000, and average annual household income is around $10,500.

Transaction volumes have fallen sharply – sales are down 44% in Xiamen. And those 20% to 40% down payments that were supposed to provide a big enough equity cushion to avoid a crash? They were borrowed. From loan sharks, no less. Speculators hoped prices would go up fast enough to cover the 60% to 100% interest. Conservative Chinese have been lending money to the loan shark pools at 3% or so a month, and the pools lent it to speculators at 5% a month.

But they've run out of greater fools. With transaction volumes down, prices will quickly follow as those who must sell get out. The speculators are going broke. That means the loan sharks are going broke, because they can't pay their lenders, the conservative Chinese. Everyone is going to go down the tubes together.

Can the government save them? Nope. The problem is too big, too widespread and too physical. The empty apartment buildings exist. There are whole purpose-built cities with no one in them. If Jim Chanos is right, there is going to be a commercial development crash of historic proportions. I guess the government could hire everyone and contract with all the construction companies to dismantle or demolish what they just finished building. But that's not likely.

Here's how they got in this mess. The government required local officials and banks to produce double-digit growth, in order to keep the potentially unemployed off the streets. Local contractors pay bribes in return for building permits and loans. The officials also take bribes to let the loan shark pools operate, so buyers can borrow the down payment. These pools are not a bunch of Mafia types, they are neighborhood, community, or church groups that act like informal credit unions. The members pool their money into a large amount and get paid 30% a year interest. Speculators then bid for use of the money month by month, with 5% per month a typical rate of interest.

Most Chinese keep a lot of cash around in case they get sick, because they have to pay their medical bills daily in cash or they get evicted from the hospital and die. Putting it to work at 30% a year is a good deal. Borrowing at 5% a month to buy an apartment that is going up in value 10% a month is a good deal. Everyone is happy until the apartment price starts to fall, and the Ponzi scheme unravels quicker than you can say "Bernie Madoff."

Local governments were encouraged to build public housing with bank loans last year, and now Premier Wen Jiabao has clamped down on real estate. Land sales to developers are falling at a rapid clip, and that money was supposed to help pay back the loans. Showrooms are empty of potential buyers, and sales volume has collapsed. These local governments are likely to assume that someone else will repay the loans, because they can't. Property-related stocks are down around 40% in the last year, close to double the drop in the Shanghai Composite Index.

The bubble has already burst. The fallout is going to be awesome, especially in a society that values "face" above almost everything else. The speculators can't sell and can't pay the loan sharks. The loan sharks not only can't pay the interest they promised, but the principal is gone. Many Chinese borrowed against the increased value of their houses to flip the proceeds into a loan shark pool at 30%, and have been living off the income. A schoolteacher who bought a house five years ago and was sitting on a quadruple was awfully tempted to pull out equity and put it in the loan shark pools, where it threw off an annual income three or four times a teacher's salary. But now their income is gone, their capital is gone, and they owe the bank more than their house is worth in a falling market.

It's not missiles and nukes like Iran, but it could be a bigger deal to the world economy. I am watching very closely as this unfolds.

Yuan Revaluation

Until the U.S. dollar begins circling the drain, China will let the yuan float up slowly. But they are going to have some immediate constraints. Even if the yuan didn't move, a lot of the Chinese manufacturers are headed for bankruptcy. They've lost too many customers in Europe, and some in the U.S., to stay in business. It's a simple question of the volume of available business. Chinese manufacturers are geared for 20% or better annual growth, and so they get extended in terms of factory space, employment levels and inventory. Yes, there is more domestic demand and, yes, the rest of Asia is buying from them – but it isn't enough. With Europe drinking the IMF Kool-Ade and putting their countries back into recession/depression, China was headed for an export struggle. An increasing yuan just makes it worse. Germany's largest export market is now China, which recently passed France. The cheap euro against the dollar was a big help to Germany, and now it will be even cheaper against the yuan.

So there will be bankruptcies and layoffs in the large export sector, which means there will be riots. There are about 100,000 serious riots a year in China now – it is a time-honored way of negotiating for something. As long as you don't try to overthrow the government, riots are somewhat tolerated. There will be many more.

The Chinese don't want the yuan to appreciate too quickly. But they also don't want to keep trading real goods for U.S. dollars that look likely to lose value – a lot of value, and possibly sooner rather than later. They know they are subsidizing American consumers and American wars. But they've been unwilling even to buy the 191.3 million tonnes of gold the IMF had left to sell in 2010, fearing they would send both gold and the yuan into orbit. If the yuan/dollar or yuan/euro relationships get away from them, there will be real chaos in the export sector, and even more riots.

The Economic Cycle

China's biggest problem may be nothing more complicated than the business cycle. Their rapid growth can blind one to the fact that they are subject to the same cycles as everyone else. Going from 10% growth to 2% growth may not be quite as painful as going from +4% to -4%, but the effects are similar. China went through a long expansion from the 1978 liberalization to about 2001, funded by domestic savings and foreign investment. Many of the drivers were simply catching up on the basics ignored by Mao and his thugs – roads, bridges, communications and so on. But by 2001, exporting was the big driver, millionaires were made overnight, and the malinvestment started.

When the rest of the world started to turn down in 2007, the Chinese were first out with a highly targeted stimulus program. Because they can tell their banks what to do, the stimulus hit their economy quickly, and it worked – they sidestepped most of the pain so far. But their stimulus resulted in a huge credit bubble; thus, the South China Mall, empty high-end apartments and the pending commercial real estate disaster. Their stock market trades at over 25x earnings, because loose money flows into financial assets first. Their stock margin requirements have been snugged up a bit, but plenty of Chinese play – and they do "play" – the market on margin.

So this has all the characteristics of the spike top of a business cycle, with overinvestment in real estate and the stock market, just as the economic underpinnings (exports) are going to weaken.

The Bottom Line

A real estate bust was coming in China even before the new yuan policy. So even if there is less yuan revaluation than the

U.S. Congress would like, there's going to be some chaos and hard times in China. Euroland's decision to cut spending will make the contraction in China's export sector noticeably more painful.

It's also very possible that the commodities boom is over for a while. China has been a big buyer at the margin, and may have stockpiled quite a bit of copper and other metals. Base metals and their stocks will suffer if China starts regurgitating inventories.

Hard times in China will hurt German exports, but the real hits will be in Brazil and Australia. Even though the new Australian Prime Minister quickly killed the 40% tax on minerals exports that the last Prime Minister backed, which led to his ouster, if China doesn't need more coal and iron ore for a while, the Aussies and Brazilians are going to feel it.

If this plays out as I expect, China will use some of their dollar foreign reserves to cover internal needs, and maybe disappear for a while from the U.S. Treasury auctions. That will be bad news for U.S. interest rates and the dollar. Rates are headed much higher and the dollar much lower, anyway, even if Bernanke can avoid a hyperinflation. China's problems are likely to make things happen sooner and bigger.

When will all this happen? It's probably starting now. If so, it will become obvious to Wall Street by the middle of 2011. I don't have a special insight here – I just know that from the time I find out Jim Chanos is shorting something to when it's clearly falling apart is about a year, and Jim went public in November 2009.

CHAPTER 10

Who Wins?

*If you know how to spend less than you get,
you have the philosopher's stone.*
—Benjamin Franklin

You can make an argument that in a hyperinflation, no one wins. It is true that if we get into hyperinflation, almost everyone will be hurt in the ensuing chaos. But "almost everyone" is not everyone, and the next chapter is about the moves you have to make to win if Bernanke loses control and we spiral into a hyperinflation.

But what about regular, high inflation? Here, there definitely are winners, and they are on the other side of the trade or deal from the losers in Chapter 10. First, those who hold assets will see them skyrocket in value. The richest 1% of households hold 33% of the assets in the U.S., and they will be fine. Stocks, investment real estate, home equity, trusts, farms and miscellaneous assets make up about 52% of their wealth, and all should go up dramatically in a high inflation.

However, about 43% of their wealth is unincorporated businesses. How those businesses do depends on how much pricing power each business has, how quickly it turns its inventory and how much fixed-rate debt it carries. The wealthy also have about 5% of their wealth in bonds, which should be called "certificates of confiscation" in a high-inflation environment. I expect you will see the wealthy dump their bonds onto the late-comer to the 28-year-old bond rally, John Q. Public. Individuals have been bailing out of equity mutual funds and buying bond mutual funds at an amazing clip. Just as they dumped their value stocks to buy dotcoms at the peak. Or sold their house in 2004 with 12 years left on their 30-year fixed-rate mortgage to buy a McMansion with a no-down, no-doc negative amortization adjustable rate mortgage. They are making their third tragic mistake in 10 years, a remarkable record of financial self-destruction.

The poor have no such worries. They don't own bonds, or anything else. The lowest percentiles have a negative net worth, and the bottom 20% have a combined net worth of zero. How they do in the Great Inflation depends on how quickly their income can increase. For example, someone paid a percentage commission on the sale of an item that is desperately needed and constantly being marked up in price might keep up, even if they have little or no net worth. But most who work for a salary or day rates are likely to find that pay increases come nowhere near matching the rate of inflation, and they will not "catch up" in a standard of living sense for years, if ever.

In general, anyone with flexible pricing on their income source, such as retailers, month-to-month rent payments or personal billing rates should be OK.

What to Own? First, a House – or Several Houses.

Stocks are up sharply from the March 2009 bottom, gold and silver are up – what is the last cheap asset class?

Real estate. Sure, in most parts of the country, it is still in the toilet. There are a lot of foreclosures still to come, many among prime loans as opposed to the subprime and Alt-A junk that is already blowing up. The percentage of 90-day delinquencies is over 9%, near the highest level recorded since the FDIC started tracking the data 26 years ago.

Apartment owners in Los Angeles are pocketing the rents, stopping maintenance, not paying the mortgage for nine months or so, and walking away with whatever they can, including the tenants' security deposits.

Commercial real estate is soft, whether office buildings or retail, as companies cut the fat. The owners of commercial real estate leveraged up to a remarkable degree, considering they are supposed to be professionals, and now face debt repayment schedules they can't meet. There will be $1 trillion in bank loan and commercial-mortgage-backed bond defaults over the next three years.

No doubt about it, real estate is a disaster. The blood is running in the streets.

Time to buy!

Real estate always is a local market, and different cities, neighborhoods and individual houses will bottom at different times. But you have three great advantages to buying today:

1. Desperate sellers. Not the homeowners, they already know they are toast and, like the apartment owners, simply stopped paying the mortgage so they would have the money for first, last and a security deposit on their next residence, a rental. It is the banks that financed them that are desperate. Everyone in the workout department has stacks of folders on their desks, their credenza, the floor – everywhere – all needing attention yesterday.

2. Little competition. Most people don't have the patience and energy to push through a pre-foreclosure, short sale offer, or a post-foreclosure real estate owned (REO) offer. Most real estate agents don't want to work that hard to get a deal done. I advised an assisted living home trying to buy a second home/facility on a short sale, and for the reasons discussed below, it was very difficult and ultimately fell through.

3. Low financing rates. If you believe major inflation is coming, at least double-digits with a real possibility of hyperinflation, getting 4-to-1 to 32-to-1 leverage at a low fixed rate of interest is like having someone *give* you money. More on this below.

Most of you will think I am way early on this recommendation, but remember that in the fall of 2008, people thought the corporate bond market would never recover. It is up dramatically from the lows. In February 2009, people thought the stock market was dead for years to come. It is up dramatically from the lows. Today they think housing will never recover. San Francisco and Miami house prices are down 47%. Phoenix and Las Vegas are down 55% to 60%. It's been brutal.

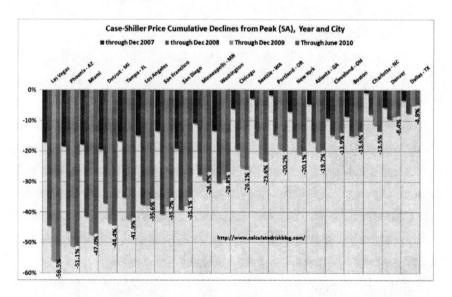

But, of course, that's exactly what makes a bottom. And remember that you can make $500,000 TAX-FREE in as little as two years by buying and living in a short sale or REO home, while renting out your current home, and then sell the foreclosure and move back into your current place. Do I have your attention?

The holiday season is the perfect time of year to make a low-ball bid on a distressed situation. Heck, if Treasury Secretary Geithner bought a Long Island house for 4.1X the $381,000 a year he made as head of the New York Fed, he was a subprime borrower. And now if he can't sell it, maybe you could give him a low-ball bid. He only makes $191,000 a year now as Secretary of the Treasury, and he can't afford to maintain two homes on half his old salary. Put him out of his misery.

According to RealtyTrac.com, there are two million foreclosure homes for sale, with a recent average selling price of $175,000. In August 2010, banks repossessed over 95,000 homes, a new record that was 25% higher than the year before. Two-thirds of all home sales today are foreclosures or short sales.

The heat map below shows that foreclosures are everywhere, but far more intense in in some areas than others:

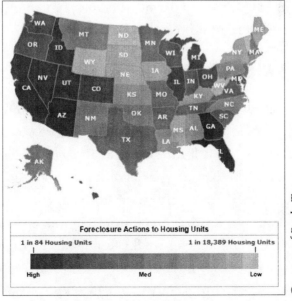

Courtesy of RealtyTrac.com

I've shown the top states below; you can find the whole list at http://www.realtytrac.com/trendcenter/.

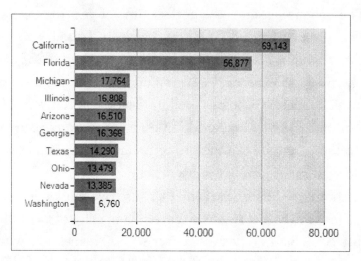

In addition, there are about 500,000 REO-homes that are not on the market yet, for various reasons. This shadow inventory, plus the shadow foreclosures coming as all the voluntary forbearances by the banks expire, means the buyers' market will continue for maybe another year. About 3% of all homes, or two million units, are sitting vacant right now. It is time to bottom-fish.

Buying A Short-Sale

A short sale is usually the most attractive way to buy distressed property, but it's also the most uncertain. Before the actual foreclosure, you make an offer to buy the property for less than the mortgage loan. The homeowner agrees for three reasons: (1) it is less of a hit to their credit report to have the house go in a short sale than in a formal foreclosure; (2) you can agree to let them stay an extra couple of weeks to find another place, rather than getting a three-day notice from the lender after foreclosure; and, (3) you can offer to pay their moving expenses or buy some of their personal property (appliances, yard equipment, DSL modem, whatever) on the condition they don't trash the place before you move in.

A troubled lender like Countrywide (now Bank of America) or Washington Mutual (now Chase) will usually take an offer equal to 80% of the loan without any argument. At 60% of the loan, they might say yes and they might say no. It depends when the loan was made. Obviously, if you are looking at a property where the borrowers paid top dollar at the peak of the market and got a 100% loan, you might have to offer as low as 20% to 30% of the loan to get a good deal. But even at that level, in some markets like Las Vegas, Phoenix or Miami, your offer will get serious consideration.

In general, start with a very low-ball offer and make them come back to you with a counter-offer. The process will take seemingly forever, and you need permission from the current borrowers to let you or your agent contact the short sale department directly. WaMu/Chase's short sale people obviously were hired off the street for $10 an hour just to deal with the flood of paper, and most of them sound like they are 22 years old and still live with their parents. They have little or no knowledge about real estate, so be prepared for a frustrating experience. The borrowers will have to submit a financial statement and a cover letter explaining why they can't pay the mortgage, and the lender will lose these at least twice and then announce the financial statement has gone out of date, and they need a new one.

Also, the short sale people do not talk to the foreclosure people, who are something like an army of locusts mindlessly marching through a wheat field. Most likely, about three days before the foreclosure sale, the short sale people will panic and accept your low bid.

Be sure you have a clear understanding with some motivation like money to be sure the current owners tell you all the problems and don't trash the house. Always have a short sale inspected by a contractor. Always have a lawyer double-check legal and insurance information, like flood zones. These seller will be long gone and probably judgment proof (= no money) if you find some major undisclosed problem later. Leave plenty of time for closing the deal. Don't fall in love with a property just because it's cheap. Or for any other reason.

The REO Sale

Except for lenders who have such a huge problem that they have had to get organized to deal with it, like Countrywide, the REO people are no better than the short sale folks. Their plan seems to be: Price the house high, wait for someone to buy it, if nobody buys it, don't cut the price until it is vandalized or mold develops. Then slash the price to the value of the land and move it out. In your or your agent's very first encounter with them, always say: "What about the mold issue?" It freaks them out.

Not many REOs are a good deal when they first come on the market. But after a few months with no offers, someone in the REO department might be willing to look at your low-ball offer and make a counteroffer. It might be helpful for your agent to do some comps with other foreclosure sales in the area that have actually closed. No matter what, it is going to take a long time. A step in the normal process that a title company would do in a day takes two or three weeks.

Banks won't give you a disclosure statement, either, so everything I said above about inspections and legal advice goes double for an REO.

That $500,000 Tax-Free Profit

Of course, I am talking about the husband and wife exclusion for the tax on the capital gain of a primary residence in which they have lived at least two of the prior five years. If you are not buying your own retirement home or something to rent to the kids, you can make the new house your primary residence (utility bills, driver's license address, income tax return, voter registration, etc.), live there two years and then sell it. To make the full $500,000, you'll have to buy something nicer than the $150,000 house on a suburban lot, and get a heck of a deal. I have noticed that some good-sized houses on golf courses have gone into foreclosure, with the last transaction price maybe $800,000 and a $640,000 mortgage. If you buy that for 35% off, you pay $416,000. When inflation takes off, you sell it for $975,000, take your half a million, give the renters of your current house 30 days notice, and go home. Not a bad deal.

The $8,000 First-Time Buyers Tax Credit

This credit expired in 2010, but I think it could be revived to help clear the wave of foreclosures coming in 2011. It may be broadened to include all homebuyers. I don't think it will be raised to $15,000, as the industry has asked for.

A first-time homebuyer is someone who has not owned a home for three years. If only you are on your current title, your spouse may be a first time homebuyer. If your kids will need a house somewhere soon, maybe they can buy it in their name with you cosigning.

A first-time homebuyer also can get a 3% down mortgage from the FHA, which has a $460,000 loan limit most places, and higher limits in expensive markets. So your wife or kids might be able to buy a $500,000 condo for $250,000 in Miami, put $7,500 down, and collect $8,000 from a new Obama stimulus program. Hey, did they just pay you $500 to take it off their hands?

Finding A Short Sale or REO

Most short sales are listed with a broker for sale, so just going to your local MLS service and using "short sale" as a search term should turn them up. You can use a service like RealtyTrac.com to identify properties that are in pre-foreclosure, and try to approach the owners with an attitude of helping them solve their problem. Just remember that they are getting bombarded by con men and will assume you are one of them at first.

Most REOs that are ready to be sold also will be listed with a realtor, often with the notations "REO," "bank-owned," or "lender-owned." There are a lot more REOs than are listed for sale, though, and if you can get through to the REO department of your local banks or find their website, you may be able to do a deal before the listing. You can also track properties right through the foreclosure process by finding out what local government office is responsible for the actual sale, and then approach the lender after the fore-closure sale but before the lender gets around to listing it with a broker. This is only worth doing when there is a particular property you want and the defaulting owner won't assist for a short sale.

Don't Forget Luxury Condos

Condominiums are overbuilt and prices are especially distressed almost everywhere, but particularly in the Sunbelt. Most condos do not allow investment buyers, so the competition to buy one often is nonexistent. Unsold luxury condos, many sitting for well over a year, have brought many builders to bankruptcy court and lenders to the courthouse steps to foreclose. Near Lake Tahoe, condos in Olympic Village, CA have been on the market an average of 461 days, and in Tahoe City, CA, 413 days. There are 38 months of supply in Seattle, 21 months in Minneapolis, and 14 months in Boston. New condos on the Upper West Side in Manhattan average 273 days on the market. Malibu has 21 condos for sale that average 306 days on the market. Dallas (Highland Park) has 36 condos that average 333 days. Lake Forest, IL has 21 condos that average 283 days.

Florida is a wipe-out. There are places in Florida where a nice condo costs less than a car. If you've ever thought of retiring to Fisher Island (350 days), Bal Harbour (285 days) or Key Biscayne (95 condos, 284 days) – or most anywhere else in the state – now is your time to act. Make a lowball offer on a luxury condo, bring all cash if possible, or a big enough down payment to qualify for a government sponsored loan, and make it your permanent residence for the next two years. Heck, you may even decide to keep it.

In addition to an income that can respond to inflation and owning assets, winners will leverage their assets with fixed rate debt. As long as they are sure they can cover the monthly interest payment, getting leveraged or even highly leveraged is a smart way to deal with inflation. The value of the assets rises while the debt stays the same, with a leveraged impact on your net worth. Even adjustable rate debt might help if the annual and lifetime interest rate caps are low enough.

Second, Buy Two Kinds of Stocks

Paul Volker was appointed Chairman of the Federal Reserve in August 1979 by President Jimmy Carter. Faced with an accelerating inflation with both cost-push elements from oil prices and demand-pull elements from loose money, he started raising interest rates. By January 1980 the economy was in a recession that lasted through July. But inflation didn't peak until 1981, at 13.5%. So Volker kept the pressure on and raised the Fed funds rate to 20% in June 1981. That sent the economy into a second recession that lasted from July 1981 to November 1982. That month, at the bottom of the second recession, Carter lost the 1982 election to Ronald Reagan, who then reappointed Volker as Fed Chairman in 1983.

During almost all of this time, the stock market was in the dumps. I started the *California Technology Stock Letter* in January 1982, and by August the prices of tech stocks were so ridiculously low I wrote an issue that essentially said: "I don't know why stocks are this cheap, but mortgage the farm and go all in <u>now</u>." That was on Friday, August 13, 1982, and it turned out the market bottom was the day before.

Since then, the bond market has been in a 28-year bull market. Inflation came down from 20% to nothing. So for most Americans, including many of my fellow newsletter writers, accelerating inflation = bad stock market. Right now, I see lots of people, mostly bears, clinging to the idea of deflation. They will be proven totally wrong. But what drives me nuts is the number of people who do see the inflation coming, maybe even hyperinflation, and then say "get out of stocks now." The early 1980s is all they know.

But what brought stocks down then was not the inflation, it was Volker having the guts to raise rates so high. Wikipedia says: "Volcker's Fed elicited the strongest political attacks and most widespread protests in the history of the Federal Reserve (unlike any protests experienced since 1922), due to the effects of the high interest rates on the construction and farming sectors, culminating in indebted farmers driving their tractors onto C Street NW and blockading the Eccles Building."

In today's political environment, given Bernanke's fear and loathing of deflation, do you think he'll raise rates that high? Does President Obama want to go into the 2012 election with a 21.5% prime rate? I don't think so, unless he craves a career change to building houses for Habitat for Humanity. Bernanke is no Volker, and not only are we in for high inflation, there's a pretty good chance the Fed will lose control of the situation. Just as the international bond vigilantes decided one week to give up on Greece, the dollar could fall *or be pushed* into a sudden plunge that the Fed can't stop without taking drastic, Volker-like action. And why should they do that, when they can blame the markets or China or George Soros or whoever they want for attacking the dollar and causing a high inflation that just happens to make it much easier for the U.S. government to repay its debts?

So what happens to stocks when a country can't or won't deal with its inflation? In Germany in January 1919, their stock market index was at 99. Inflation began and by January 1920, the index was up to 166, up 67% in one year. Inflation and the stock market continued up, right to the top in January 1925 at

26,890,000

Of course, there was a deflationary crash after that, and stocks collapsed. They do that in a *de*flation. But in the *in*flation they rose and protected people's real wealth, because stocks are part-ownership in real assets – buildings, machinery, patents, products, distribution systems – and real assets go up in an inflation. Precious metals, commodities, stocks and even real estate will protect you when the dollar hits the fan.

The same thing happened in Argentina. That country has been the scene of several hyperinflations, with the circulating currency replaced every so often by a new currency that typically offers one new peso for 10,000 to 1,000,000 old pesos. Most recently, in January 2002 the appointed President, Eduardo Duhalde, abandoned the fixed 1-to-1 peso/dollar parity that had been in place for 10 years. In just a few days, a provisional exchange rate of 1.4 pesos per dollar was set, and all bank accounts denominated in dollars were converted to pesos. After a few months, the 1.4-to-1 ratio was abandoned and the peso left to float...or, rather, sink like a stone. Inflation hit 10.4% *per month* in April 2002, and business was collapsing. By the end of 2002 the peso/dollar ratio was down 80% to almost 4-to-1. The unemployment rate hit nearly 25% in 2003, and thousands of people were homeless, living by scavenging cardboard off the streets. After a new election in early 2003, President Nestor Kirchner took over in May and stabilized the situation. He took advantage of the dramatically devalued peso to boost Argentina's exports, while creating credit for business investment and improving tax collections. He also increased social welfare spending to get people off the streets. By December 2005, Argentina had $28 billion in foreign currency reserves and was able to pay off all its International Monetary Fund debt.

The most commonly-watched stock market index for Argentina is the Merval Buenos Aires (^MERV on Yahoo). It is only 12 large companies, but it is reasonably representative. Here's how it did during this most recent hyperinflation:

12/28/2001	272.76	Begin
1/2/2002	323.69	Duhalde abandons peso/dollar parity
1/4/2002	343.22	Stock market closes for eight days; 1.4-to-1 peso/dollar ratio set
4/30/2002	387.79	Peso left to float; monthly inflation hits 10.1%
12/31/2002	525.95	Peso down 80% to 4-to-1
4/30/2003	635.95	Unemployment hits 25%

5/5/2003   653.67   President Kirchner sworn in
12/31/2003 1,071.95 Situation stabilized
12/31/2004 1,375.37 Argentina well on the road to recovery
12/29/2005 1,543.31 Argentina has $28 billion in foreign
                                  exchange reserves to pay off IMF debt

Through all the chaos, currency devaluation, hyperinflation and economic hardship from 2002 on, here's a chart of how the Merval protected shareholders through the end of 2004:

This is what normally happens in a rapid inflation or hyper-inflation. Stocks don't sell based on their earnings, which may disappear from time to time as they get caught with no inventory due to supply chain disruptions, or customers are so confused by currency changes that they freeze up. Stocks sell on the basis of their underlying businesses, which may include hard assets like land, or intellectual property like patents, or harder-to-define advantages like airline gates and routes, goodwill, distribution systems – really, the totality of what makes any company valuable. When currency is tight, that value will track lower with the general level of deflation. When currency is available by the wheelbarrow, that value will soar with inflation or hyperinflation.

Imagine all the pundits on an Argentinian version of CNBC during the market charted above, constantly explaining why the market *couldn't* go up any more because the economy was in chaos and the peso was falling. That's what you'll see during the coming Great Inflation, Ben Bernanke's legacy and bookend to the Great Depression. It isn't high inflation that causes stocks to go down, it's *fighting* inflation that causes stocks to go down. When it comes to fighting inflation, Bernanke is no Volker.

So don't get sucked in to the accelerating inflation = bad stock market "analysis" you are going to hear. It's not just Gold, Guns and Gardens you'll need during the coming unpleasantness. Stocks, Silver and a Subprime Short-Sale should be in your portfolio, too.

The Business Cycle

Economies go into hyperdrive, inflation picks up, stock prices climb, the Fed takes away the punchbowl, stock prices fall six months before the economy slows, inflation falls, the Fed creates a stock market bottom by switching to monetary expansion, the economy recovers, and then goes into hyperdrive. Rinse and repeat. That's the business cycle.

The reason bear market troughs occur during inflationary periods is that's when the Fed tightens the screws. But during the period of expansion and accelerating inflation, stocks do an excellent job of hedging against inflation.

Sure, if Paul Volker is Secretary of the Treasury, you are going to get the serious tightening required to stop runaway inflation. He was appointed in August 1979 and served until early 1987. (See chart on next page)

So during a very inflationary time, stocks fell. But the question is, would Bernanke do what Volker did? Would the Obama

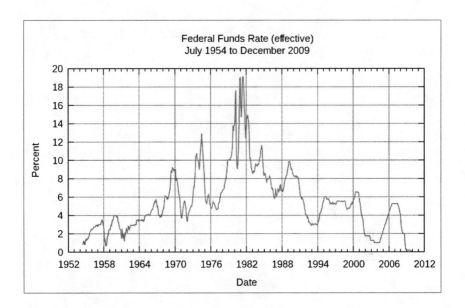

Administration let him? Even further, is the entire system in Washington now so different that no one would be able to "do a Volker" again? I am afraid so.

What Are the Two Kinds of Stocks You Should Buy?

First, a little background. Pundits say 67% of Americans are overweight, of which 40% are obese. But if they want to visit ground zero for fat tails, they have to go to Wall Street. You undoubtedly are familiar with the bell-shaped curve of a normal distribution. The middle is the median and average, and the further away from the middle you get, the less likely it is that you will find anything happening. (See chart next page)

Almost every academic article on the stock market, the capital market pricing model, efficient market theory or the random walk theory starts off: "Assume stock prices are normally distributed." But guess what? Stock prices are not normally distributed. Not

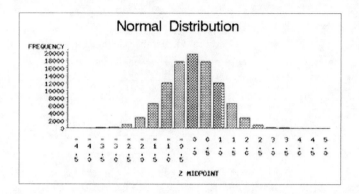

even close. There are far too many extremely good and extremely bad events. This is a chart of the daily logarithmic return on the Dow Jones Industrial Average for 80 years, from 1928 to 2008:

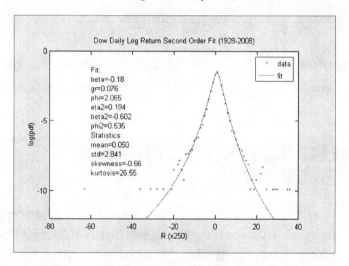

The academic name for this kind of distribution is "stable Paretian distribution with a characteristic exponent less than 2." The popular name is "fat-tailed distribution." There are too many outlier events – "black swans" – relative to what you would expect in a normal distribution.

This is important because the statistical methods that work on normal distributions mostly do not work on a stable Paretian distribution. For example, regression doesn't work. If someone "assumes" stock prices are normally distributed and then uses regression analysis to calculate the beta of a stock, or an alpha, or an efficient portfolio – that is all garbage. Long Term Capital Management had not one but two Nobel-prize winning economists who helped develop modern capital market theory using standard statistical analysis assuming a normal distribution. Their game plan was to exploit small discrepancies in asset pricing by leveraging up 100-to-1. It worked great until Russia defaulted on its debt – an event that might be represented by the leftmost red dot in the graphic above. Overnight, Long Term Capital Management was bust.

Fat-tailed distributions are important to you, too, because the way you have been told to structure your portfolio and manage your risk is wrong. It never was right, but it *seemed* right as long as everything was more or less O.K., and it fit academic thinking based on the capital asset pricing model.

You were told to think of your portfolio as a pyramid. At the base are low-risk, low-return assets like bonds, preferably governments. Then maybe a smaller layer of riskier convertible bonds, or a mutual fund or exchange-traded fund (ETF) that holds them. Then an even smaller layer of blue chip, dividend paying stocks, or an index fund. John Bogle of Vanguard or Burton Malkiel of *A Random Walk Down Wall Street* will be quick to tell you that the stock market is efficient, no one can outperform it reliably, so your best bet is an index fund. I'd love to see them give that presentation to the Goldman Sachs proprietary trading desk, or some of the deep-value hedge funds that have beaten the market for 30 years.

Finally, almost at the top of the pyramid, are small-cap stocks, development-stage biotech and other companies, junior gold miners and the like. At the very top, the tiniest point, are options. Most financial advisers will tell you to ignore both of these layers.

Two Big Problems

There are two big problems with their advice, which are a direct result of fat-tailed distributions. First, it is very hard to control your *absolute* risk this way. Sure, you can control your *relative* risk by shifting some money at the margins back and forth from cash to bonds to stocks. But then along comes 2008, a black swan, fat-tailed event if there ever was one, and everything goes to hell. People's retirement portfolios get killed. They had no idea they were taking that much absolute risk, and *neither did their financial advisers who are still living in a normal distribution world.*

Second, that advice can't generate enough returns over the coming five or ten or 20 years to give someone a comfortable retirement. Using their capital markets, risk/return analysis to manage your portfolio going forward can't get you to where you want to be, so why do it? But if the pyramid model is based on faulty statistics and won't get you where you want to go, what should you do?

Be a Barbell Investor, Not A Dumbbell Investor

I think relying on clearly faulty statistics is dumb. Anyone who talks to you about beta, alpha, statistical diversification, efficient portfolios or index funds is just making it up. Your only defense is to view your portfolio as a barbell. On one end should be extremely safe, high yield investments that will give you a fighting chance against inflation, deflation or whatever comes, with very little risk of blowing up. That might be 80% to 95% of your whole portfolio, depending on where you are in your investment life cycle. So one end of your portfolio has very low or no risk, and you are going to let that high yield compound right into and through retirement.

At the other end should be a small allocation to high-risk investments that will pay off huge if they work out. Not too many of them, with not much money invested in each one. *And nothing in the middle.* That's right, no index funds, no blue-chip mutual funds, no junk bond funds, no diversified funds…nothing. You *know* the risk in the safe end of your portfolio is very, very low. You *know* the risk in the other end of your portfolio is very, very high. You control your overall risk by moving a little money from one end of the barbell to the other, because when you don't own anything in the middle, it only takes a small shift between the two ends of the barbell to make a big difference in your overall risk.

On balance, most of you will wind up with a medium-risk portfolio. But unlike the other guy's collection of mutual funds, blue-chip stocks and ETFs, you will actually know how much risk you are taking. That is about 90% of the battle for investment survival.

What Goes In The Safe Investments?

Cash in the form of U.S. dollars in Citibank is not a safe investment. U.S. 30 year bonds are not a safe investment. They would both be hurt badly by high inflation. You have to "stress test" your portfolio under a wide variety of scenarios, including the fat-tail extreme scenarios of hyperinflation and Great Depression deflation. It's like the 100-year floods in the Midwest that seem to come every 10 years these days – there are things you might do or insurance you might buy for an every-10-year-flood that you wouldn't bother with for an every-100-year flood. The world's current economic systems are more fragile, if not unstable, right now, and probably will be for the next few years. So the likelihood of a "black swan" or fat-tail event is higher than usual.

What's safe in this environment is a small number of deep-value and/or high-yield securities of global multinationals and financially solid smaller companies. There are several ways to find them. One way is to look at what other successful investors with a long-term track record are doing. My favorite way to do that is to look at the SEC 13F form filed quarterly by the major private equity funds, focusing on those filed by the deep-value funds like Greenlight Capital's David Einhorn, Baupost's Seth Klarman and Appaloosa's David Tepper. You can assemble a portfolio of the biggest new high-yield holdings from three or four funds and just coattail them. Find the filings at http://www.sec.gov/edgar/ searchedgar/webusers.htm. At this writing they hold stocks like Bank of America, Wells Fargo, Pfizer, Hartford Financial Services, Breitburn Energy Partners, News Corp., Cardinal Health, CareFusion and Foster Wheeler.

You also could look at conservative, income-oriented newsletters like my friend Richard Band's *Profitable Investing*, Jim Stack's *InvesTech Research*, Dan Ferris' *Extreme Value*, Tom Dyson's *12% Letter*, or Bryan Perry's *25% Cash Machine*.

Not everything these newsletters recommend is suitable for your ultra-safe money, but it isn't hard to pick out the recommendations that fit the bill.

There are several types of investments that are target-rich environments for high yields. As a general rule, the reason these opportunities exist is that institutions don't buy them, either for legal reasons or because the sector is too small to make it worth analyzing. Without a large number of buyers, Wall Street won't pay analysts to follow these investments. So things get mispriced. In addition to the free SEC EDGAR system, QuantumOnline. com is free but requires registration. It offers unbiased information on preferred stocks and other exchange-traded securities such as real estate investment trusts (REITS), closed-end mutual funds, exchange-traded funds (ETFs), and royalty trusts.

What Goes In The "Pay Off Huge" Investments?

The idea here is to take higher risks with a small amount of money on an event that, if it does occur, will make you a large amount of money. For example, you could buy far out of the money two-year puts on the euro, betting that the Eurozone will break up over the next two years as Spain, Italy, Belgium and Ireland follow Greece down the tubes. Or you could buy far out of the money calls on hyperinflation by using silver or gold.

Using options, you could short the S&P 500 and go long gold, or short the 30-year U.S. Treasury bond, and stay short as long as Tim Geithner and Ben Bernanke have a government job.

My favorite places for the "pay off huge" portion of a portfolio are development-stage biotech and medtech companies, under-followed (often completely unfollowed) technology stocks, and junior gold miners. That's because I understand the first two areas, and I only invest in junior miners that have a proven, trustworthy management team. Also, the stocks I recommend usually are so depressed, sometimes by naked short-selling, that I'm not likely to lose any money. My risk is more that nothing happens for a long time.

This is the intellectual underpinning for my Recovery Trade Strategy, starting with only $2,000. I have to pick four big winners in a row, with the profits from one rolled into the next, and each stock has to be available at an attractive price when its turn in the rotation comes up. Not so easy and the odds are against it, but… you only risk $2,000 to make as much as $1 million, and the rest of your money is safely collecting dividends or interest.

Investors damaged by the various bear markets over the last decade need to get to very safe ground with most of their assets. Nobody knows what's coming next. But those same investors need to deploy a small amount of money into a few potentially very high return situations if they are to have any hope of recovering their losses and moving on to acquire enough assets to hit their targeted needs. That's the barbell strategy, and it is the best way I see to control your risk while getting to your objective.

CHAPTER 11

Hard Assets

(I AM NOT A GOLD BUG, BUT...)

Where there's no law, there's no bread.

—Benjamin Franklin

ard assets include gold, silver and other precious metals, base metals like copper, forest products and similar essential goods. The agricultural commodities like wheat are not usually considered hard assets, but their prices probably will track those of hard assets in the Great Inflation, especially a hyperinflation.

Aside from the twin dolphins wedding ring on my left hand, I don't have an emotional attachment to gold. Never wore a lot of gold jewelry, never collected gold coins. I did take my older kids panning for gold at Sutter's Mill one time, and got a big kick out of watching them get gold fever and elbow each other for "the best spot," which meant wherever the last flake of gold showed up. I also never recommended investing in gold until February 5, 2009, in the first *Radar Report* I wrote after I took over *New World Investor* from InvestorPlace Media. I had been eager to make that recommendation for months, because it became obvious as the subprime housing/banking/Wall Street catastrophe unfurled that the Federal Reserve System wanted us to buy gold.

Now, Chairman Bernanke never stood at a podium and said: "You'd better buy gold if you know what's good for you." I wouldn't expect him to do that, and it wasn't necessary anyway. All he had to do was show us the Fed's balance sheet, and say he was going to follow a policy of "quantitative easing." "Quantitative" = "Money." "Easing" = "Print." "Print Money" was all I needed to hear to pull the trigger on my gold and silver recommendations, and a month later the whole market took off as the newly-printed money started flowing into financial assets.

Gold & Silver

Money is classically defined as something that can act as a medium of exchange, a store of value, a unit of account and a standard of deferred payment. A medium of exchange is needed to avoid the inconvenience of barter, where each person has to want exactly what the other person has to trade. In order to be a medium of exchange, the item used as money does not need to have any inherent value of its own. That's why paper money works. It could have inherent value, like salt or spices used as money in the past. But whatever is used as a medium of exchange does have to be transportable, divisible, have a high market value in relation to its volume and weight, and be recognizable and resistant to counterfeiting.

In addition, to be a store of value it should be inert, and not tarnish or rust over time, or lose weight. Thus, salt was a pretty good form of money as long as it didn't get wet. Some spices lose their potency over time. Gold and silver don't tarnish, and were widely used as money in the past. Precious stones work as a store of value, but are hard to value as a medium of exchange.

A "unit of account" simply means a unit for accounting – dollars, ounces of gold, or whatever. Typically, this is currency, which may or may not be exchangeable into gold. A "standard of deferred payment" means a unit for a debt that will be paid in the future. Again, currency is most common, although there is no reason it could not be ounces of gold or silver, or anything else two parties agree to.

So how do paper money, gold and silver rate on these requirements? Paper money is an excellent medium of exchange. It is very transportable and divisible – it's easy to make change. It has a very high market value in relation to its volume and weight, and it certainly is recognizable and resistant to counterfeiting. As a store of value, in and of itself it is terrible. It is simply too tempting for whoever issues the paper money to print more and more of it, so they can consume a higher percentage of the resources available to society. If it is backed by gold or silver, it then becomes a good store of value.

Gold is not a good medium of exchange for small transactions, but silver is pretty good. Both are transportable. Both are divisible down to about ¼ ounce, but below that it is better to use a base metal (nickel or copper) and just assign it the lower values. Gold has a very high market value in relation to its weight at $1300 an ounce, although nowhere near paper money. Silver also has a high market value around $21 an ounce. While both are recognizable, it is easier to counterfeit them, as many purchasers of "gold" bars from non-reputable sources may find out. Gold coins, though, are harder to counterfeit and at least carry heavy penalties for anyone who gets caught trying. As a store of value, both are superb. You have undoubtedly heard the standard story that an ounce of gold would buy a fine man's suit in 1913 and still will today, while $20.67 in paper money in 1913 won't even get you a decent leather belt today.

So paper money is better as a medium of exchange, and gold and silver are better as a store of value. The obvious best solution is paper money backed 100% by gold, which is where we were prior to April 5, 1933. On that day, President Franklin Roosevelt issued Executive Order 6102 "forbidding the Hoarding of Gold Coin, Gold Bullion, and Gold Certificates" by U.S. citizens. The Order required U.S. citizens to deliver, on or before May 1, 1933, all but a small amount of gold coin, gold bullion, and gold certificates owned by them to the Federal Reserve, in exchange for $20.67 per troy ounce. Once the citizens sold their gold to the Fed for $20.67 per troy ounce, the government raised the price of gold to $35 an ounce. Oddly enough, people did not take to the streets, tar and feather the rascals and throw them all out of office. It was a gentler time.

Gold did not really go up in inherent value. The dollar went down – it was devalued against gold. Since that fateful day, it has been devalued a lot more. Now, with the U.S. national public debt growing about $4 billion a *day* to $13+ trillion, and total U.S. debt including unfunded Social Security and Medicare benefits around $75 trillion or $250,000 for every American, the dollar can never get more valuable except on a transient basis. Since 1960, the number of dollars in circulation has increased by 50 times, and between September 3, 2008, and December 31, 2008, the monetary base of the United States rose from less than $895 billion to more than $2.218 trillion, a 148% rise in less than four months.

The dollar has lost 42% of its value just since 2001. That's why the United Nations and foreign governments are seriously considering replacing the dollar as the world's reserve currency with a basket of currencies. With the euro in even worse shape, that talk has died down, but I expect it to be revived when Europe stabilizes.

Gold normally trades like a commodity, with a stable (actually slowly declining) supply and fluctuating demand, depending on how much money India and China have to spend on jewelry. But when investors lose confidence in currencies, there is an extra demand for gold. If they lose confidence in a major currency, because the pool of gold is so much smaller than the pool of currencies, demand for gold can for all intents and purposes become unlimited. With the dollar, euro and yen in a race for the bottom, it is easy to predict panic buying of gold at some point. It's a lot harder to predict the timing.

But hasn't the panic buying already occurred? Isn't gold at $1300 an ounce already in or – heaven forefend – at the top of a bubble? Probably not. The chart below shows the 1970s bull market and bubble in green, and the 1999 to present bull market in red. The most recent run from $300 in 1999 does not look like a volatile panic, it is just up-and-to-the-right steady accumulation:

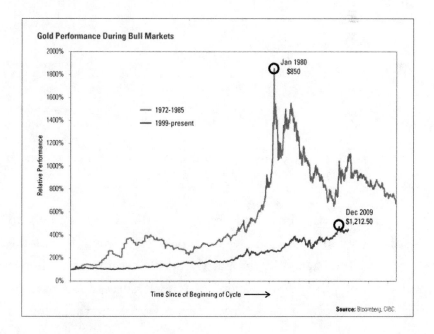

In the 1970s run, investment demand peaked around 27 million ounces as people tried to protect themselves from double-digit inflation. Investment demand today is more than double that, thanks in large part to gold becoming a legitimate asset class with exchange-traded funds and more gold-based mutual funds from the large fund companies. At the same time, the developing world is much more affluent, and people there are used to holding gold to store their wealth. That attitude even pervades the governments, as both China and India have built up their government gold holdings to diversify away from the dollar, euro and yen.

And adjusted for inflation, gold's rise has been more moderate in U.S. dollars:

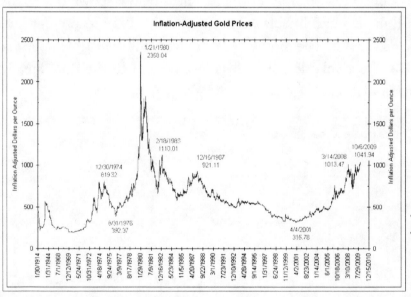

Eventually, the U.S. and the rest of the world is likely to "revalue" gold to a much higher value per ounce, and reinstate the Treasury Note backed by gold as the ideal medium of exchange *and* store of value. The current Federal Reserve notes may be converted into the new Treasury Notes at some ratio that depends on the amount of inflation that has transpired. If there is just high double-digit inflation for several years that drives the price of gold up, the conversion could be as low as 10- or 20-to-one. If Bernanke loses it and we slip into hyperinflation, the conversion could be hundreds- or thousands-to-one. Who knows? There's no way to tell in advance. It is entirely possible Federal Reserve notes will not be converted at all, with the market left to decide what they are worth compared to Treasury notes backed by gold.

How to Own Gold & Silver

In order to protect yourself and profit from the Great Inflation, you should hold gold and silver in some form. That means holding physical bullion or coins (probably not collectible or rare coins), or an exchange-traded fund like the SPDR Gold Shares (GLD) or iShares Silver Trust (SLV) that holds the physical metals, or stocks in individual gold and silver miners and royalty trusts.

I think all of these have their place. Bags of junk silver coins are bulky, but will be very useful in a hyperinflation because they are spendable in small amounts. Having three months of living expenses at current prices in junk silver (circulated pre-1964 dimes, quarters, half-dollars and dollars) is an insurance policy that should pay off no matter what happens. Gold coins and bars are wonderful stores of value, but not that useful for transactions, and tricky to store. Safe deposit box? Storage unit? Buried three feet deep in PVC pipe in the backyard, with some old metal buried at 18" to fool the metal detector? In the U.S. or offshore? I have some suggestions further on.

The exchange-traded funds are an easy way to hold gold and silver, and I am not worried about the fear that "they don't actually hold the metal." They do. They have physical audits and financial audits. Requesting delivery of the stock certificates makes your gold very transportable. It is true that gold coins won't set off a metal detector at the airport, but a sheaf of GLD or SLV certificates in your suitcase won't raise any questions, either. The major negative is that the IRS does not give capital gains treatment to these exchange-traded funds.

Remembering Mark Twain's dictum that a gold mine is a hole in the ground with a liar standing next to it, the safest way to invest in gold and silver miners is to buy something that has been vetted by industry analysts, like the Market Vectors Gold Miners ETF (GDX) or Junior Gold Miners ETF (GDXJ), or a royalty trust like Franco-Nevada (FNV.TO) or Silver Wheaton (SLW). The key to buying stock in an individual mining company is to only invest with people who have a track record of honesty and success.

Timing Your Purchases

It is important to realize that when you find a real bull market, whether it is a stock that is setting new highs every day or a class of investments like gold and silver doing the same thing, trying to trade the move rarely adds value. Almost always, the best outcome will come from buying and holding. Yes, the day will come when you have to make the decision to sell and walk away, but that is far different from trying to catch every wiggle and twist as the price works its way higher.

Having said that, not many people actually own gold today. Almost all of them – perhaps you – are worried about buying in at the top of a long move, near the highs. So can you "time" your gold and silver investments for even higher profits, or a lower cost of entry? Perhaps. Gold does well when the real rate of interest – the interest rate on 90-day Treasury bills minus inflation – on cash is low or nothing:

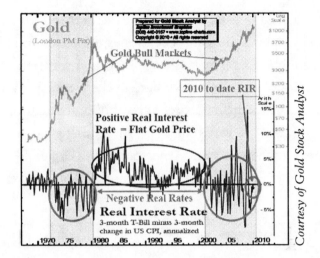

The current real interest rate is just barely negative, because reported inflation is so low. But as inflation accelerates, short-term interest rates tend to lag. Cash loses purchasing power, and people buy gold. Keeping an eye on the real interest rate can help you know when you should start or stop buying.

Silver is even more attractive than gold today, as the ratio of gold to silver is around 60x, still near its record levels. The historical norm is around 15x to 16x. In fact, silver is rising from a 700 year inflation adjusted low:

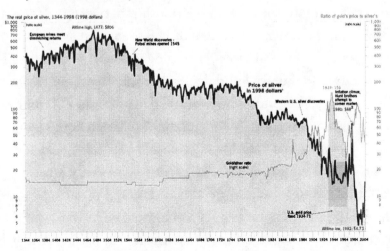

Silver also gets used up – 95% of the demand for silver is for industrial use in healthcare, cellphones, batteries and numerous other products. Little of it is reclaimed and recycled. There are no stockpiles of silver left anywhere in the world. Fifty years ago, the U.S. government held over three billion ounces of silver. By November 2000, it was gone. The government has to buy silver in the open market to mint American Silver Eagles. There's little wonder that silver has broken out over the $19.50 level to a new yearly high:

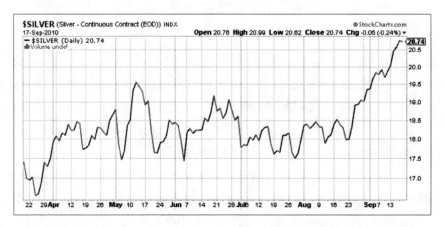

As inflation takes off, gold and silver should continue their rise. In addition to the normal relationship between inflation and gold prices, the unhappy holders of U.S. debt will swap as much of it as they can for real assets, including gold and gold mines. The International Monetary Fund decided to sell 403.3 metric tonnes of its gold in 2009, and India's central bank bought 200 tonnes of it in a single transaction. Mauritius and Sri Lanka bought another 12 tonnes. China has been buying gold and gold miners, in addition to raw materials and commodity producers of every kind.

If the Chinese economy slows down, I'm sure all these commodities they are buying, including gold and silver, would fall. Silver would probably fall more than gold, simply because it has industrial uses that would be impacted by a downturn in demand. But any such slowdown would be temporary, and the underlying growth rates of China and India alone are enough to drive gold, silver and real assets higher. Severe weakness in the dollar would drive all these assets even higher – much higher.

What is the downside for gold and silver? A three-year chart of silver shows that excepting the chaos of late 2008, buyers appear when silver falls to $12 an ounce. That number should be higher in the future to account for a weaker dollar:

Are we likely to see a test this large anytime soon? Probably not. At the margin, people who didn't want dollars in 2009 and bought euros now don't want euros or dollars, so they are buying gold and silver.

Anyone can say that gold will rise someday due to the Fed's debasement of the dollar, but the question is: Is today the day? Here's how to tell. The single best gold stock timing indicator in the world is the bullish percent index (BPI) of the gold stock sector. You want to buy when the BPI is low, typically below 30, and sell when it is running higher, up over 80, and everyone else is jumping on the train (as they are at this writing). But you also want to wait for the BPI to reverse direction before you act, because both downturns and upswings can run longer than you can stay solvent, to paraphrase Keynes:

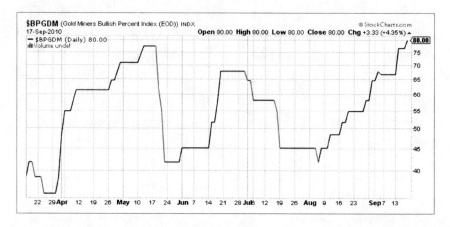

In early February 2010, gold stocks were the most oversold they'd been since late 2008. This was a great time to buy them, but we are now through the cycle and back to 80. After a late-2008 signal, the SPDR Gold Shares exchange-traded fund (GLD) doubled in four months. I would not sell core positions in gold, but if you are trading, it is time to watch prices carefully, let them run, and keep your sneakers tied for a reversal.

China & Gold

According to the World Gold Council, at the end of 2009 China was the world's sixth-largest official holder of gold at 1,054 metric tons. China also has become the largest gold producer in the world. In 2008 they produced over nine million ounces of gold, and their production is increasing while other countries' is falling.

But the government's gold holdings account for only 1.5% of their total reserves, so they have lots of room to increase purchases. On the other hand, they would completely disrupt the gold market if they tried to take gold up to a substantially higher percentage of their reserves, which now total $2.3 trillion with $1.6 trillion of that in U.S. dollars. They quickly denied rumors they would buy the rest of the IMF's gold in a single transaction, but they may be talking down gold to give them a better price to buy it on the open market. They admitted they have been quietly buying gold for the last seven years, and now hold 30 times as much as they had 20 years ago. China Investment Corp., China's sovereign wealth fund, holds $155.6 million in the SPDR Gold Shares, and no one knows what the gold investments are from Chinese private funds and investors.

The government also told their citizens that gold is a good investment, and they might think of putting 5% of their savings in gold and silver. Can you imagine Chairman Bernanke saying such a thing to Americans? Chinese can easily buy gold at banks and post offices, and China is full of official "mint stores" that manufacture and distribute gold and silver medallions and commemorative coins ("rounds"). There has not been a long history of individuals owning gold in China, as there is in India, so this is a new and potentially very large source of demand. Urban Chinese households have about $36 billion in disposable income, an average of $1,300 per household. They have no Social Security and no pensions, so saving money for retirement is a big deal.

About 9.5 million ounces of gold will be turned into medallions and rounds in 2010, worth about $11 billion or 30% of disposable income. About 35 million ounces of silver will become medallions and rounds, worth about $700 million or only 1.9% of disposable income. These medallions and rounds will be bought up and disappear from circulation. My friend Robert Hsu calls the Chinese middle class "Chuppies" – Chinese upwardly-mobile professionals. Their numbers are expected to increase by 70% by 2020, and almost all of them will become gold and silver consumers.

Although China has downplayed the idea of buying the IMF's gold, they have been encouraging domestic production, which they can buy quietly off-market, and the China Gold Association told *The China Daily* that China would buy gold directly by buying gold mines overseas. If they want to own gold miners, so might you. Look how relatively cheap they've been (although they are catching up recently):

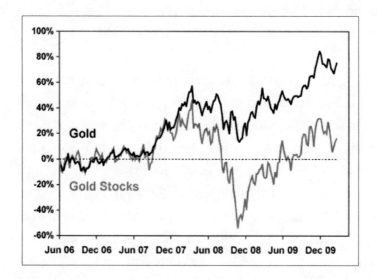

Usually the price of miners moves about twice the percentage rate as the price of gold, and that happened at the end of 2008 to the downside. Since then, until recently the miners have under-performed, and there is still lots of catching–up to do.

Ways to Buy Gold

The exchange-traded funds that actually hold gold and silver, SPDR Gold shares (GLD) and iShares Silver Trust (SLV), are treated by the IRS as investments in the underlying metals, and profits on these investments are not qualified for capital gains treatment. I recommend owning instead the exchange-traded funds that own the miners, the Market Vectors Gold Miners ETF (GDX), Market Vectors Junior Gold Miners ETF (GDXJ), and Global X Silver Miners ETF (SIL). The miners are more volatile than the price of gold, but that's a good thing in a bull market.

Owning some actual metal also makes sense. Bags of junk silver (pre-1964 dimes, quarters and half-dollars), the common gold and silver coins like the American Gold Eagle, American Silver Eagle, Canadian Maple Leaf, Canadian Silver Maple Leaf and South African Krugerrand, and even gold and silver bars will do well. You can even buy gold in an IRA, if it is 24 karat, or 22 karat American Eagles. You need to store them properly. British luxury department store Harrods now sells a full range of Swiss investment grade 999.9 fine gold bars that meet international good delivery standards. You pay what they call market-linked prices, and they will store the bars for you, too.

For storage, I recommend two home safes, one with some silver and a piece of gold that you could reluctantly tell an armed robber about under duress, and the other with the vast majority of your gold. Bank safe deposit boxes may not work out well if the banks are forced to close in a financial emergency. Overseas safe deposit boxes could be better, depending on the country. Some people rent a storage unit, and some rent a storage unit in a foreign country. I would rather use a private overseas vault like Safes Fidelity in Geneva or Das Safe in Vienna. These are the confidential vaults that are not required to be listed on your tax return, because it is the position of the IRS that gold is not money(!). You can send the overseas vaults your gold by registered, insured mail, or just take it there yourself.

Some bury their gold in their backyard inside PVC pipe, perhaps with some old metal over it to fool anyone with a metal detector. However you store it, make sure someone else knows about it, perhaps via a sealed letter with your will, and don't forget to pay the annual rent on your storage unit or safe deposit box, if any.

Gold jewelry carries too high a markup when it is new, and most investors don't want to take the time to learn how to evaluate it to buy it wholesale, used or at estate auctions. If you are into that, though, people will sell you gold at well below market prices – witness the success of MC Hammer and Ed McMahon persuading late-night TV watchers to sell their gold cheaply to Cash4Gold.

Paper gold is a certificate from a trusted source that represents direct ownership of gold kept in storage by a third party. It allows you to buy, store, sell and transport gold without having to move the physical metal. Because the government is not willing to admit that gold is money, you don't have to report the certificates as a foreign bank account. Perth Mint Certificate are held at the Perth Mint in Australia, guaranteed by the Australian government, fully insured by Lloyd's of London, and have both internal and independent audits

The downside is that you have to keep the certificates very safe – they are bearer certificates, which means the gold belongs to whoever has them. You'll have to pay a storage fee for the gold backing your certificates. And at the end of the day, if some government shows up at the door of the storage facility with tanks and says they are taking the gold, they'll get it.

Watch Out for Crooks

Buy only certified, assayed gold. Tungsten is the only lower value metal that has a specific density close enough to gold to fabricate passable counterfeit pieces of the same size and weight as genuine coins and ingots. In early 2010 the world's largest private gold refinery in Germany discovered a 500 gram bar that had the right physical dimensions and weight, but when they cut it in half, it was 99% tungsten with 1% gold plating.

China's central bank is thought to have discovered four 400-ounce gold-plated tungsten bars among those it had recently received from bonded warehouses in the United States. There are rumors that fake bars with serial numbers have even been found in Fort Knox, all coming from one smelter.

In June 2010, the SEC charged six people in a $300 million gold-based Ponzi scheme. They promised 3,000 investors that they could earn 18% to 36% a year with investments in mining companies "collateralized by gold." As gold and silver climb, the scammers will be out in force. Deal with reputable people, and don't be afraid to ask for *and check* references.

The Bottom Line: You need to own gold and silver. Start with junk silver, where you can buy a half-bag, quarter-bag or just $100 face value to keep it affordable. Or American Silver Eagles. Build up to three months of living expenses in these commodity silver coins, and then think about gold coins or bars, and silver and gold stocks.

A Note on De Facto Currency Controls

Just as patriotism is the last refuge of government scoundrels who want you to do their bidding, currency controls are the last refuge of government scoundrels who want your money. If they can't leave an economy alone to flourish, and insist on mucking it up to the point that the citizenry tries to bail out, why they'll just make it hard and/or illegal to get money or assets out of the country.

I would not be surprised if you are already thinking along these lines. It looks like the top tax rate on dividends is going up from 15% to 43.5%. Dividends are paid out of after-tax corporate income, so each dollar of pretax profits has already been taxed at 35% for Federal purposes. State tax might add another 5% to 10% to the corporate rate, and another 5% to 10% to the personal rate. So if you are in California and your company earns $1 of corporate income, you pay 35 cents to the Feds and 10 cents to the state. That leaves you 55 cents to declare as a dividend. The Feds will take about 24 cents of that from the individual, and the state will take 5.5 cents, leaving 25.5 cents for the individual. The total Federal and state income tax take is 74.5%, before you get to use your 25.5 cents to buy some gasoline, which carries Federal and state taxes to cover various highway and pollution funds, plus any state sales tax. Of course, the proposed Value-Added Tax (VAT) will be on top of all the income taxes, not a replacement of them, as the Fair Tax is (see more on the Fair Tax in Part IV) .

So, are you thinking it might be better to move some assets out of the U.S. until this nuttiness comes to its inevitable, sad conclusion? Meet the Hiring Incentives to Restore Employment (*HIRE*) *Act*, enacted March 18, 2010. Although it has nothing to do with hiring incentives, foreign financial institutions are now required to report on the investment activities of their customers who are U.S. citizens. Banks that try to protect their customers will be subjected to huge penalties on U.S.-sourced income.

I have already pointed out that you can't take more than $5 in change with you out of the country. You can't take more than $10,000 in cash without reporting it. If you have money in a foreign bank account, you must tell the government on your income tax form. If you decide to permanently relocate to a foreign country, you may have to pay your estate taxes in advance and you certainly have to continue to pay U.S. income taxes for 10 years. Of course, the U.S. is one of the few countries in the world that makes you pay taxes on money you earn outside the home country.

But the HIRE Act adds significant limitations on your freedom. Very few non-U.S. banks will be willing to do business with U.S. citizens after this. It will become much harder to hold some of your wealth outside the U.S., just at a time when that looks like a very prudent thing to do. The government is getting ready to increase taxes dramatically, and is making sure first that you can't easily move your assets and income out of reach of the IRS.

What can you own? The government's position is that gold is not money, it is a barbarous relic. So you can hold gold overseas and not report it, because it isn't a financial asset. They may change that rule next, but as of today you don't trigger any reporting requirements. It is fairly easy to buy gold in the U.S. for delivery overseas to a secure storage facility (for example, see the Perth Mint Certificate Program at http://www.perthmint.com. au/investment_certificate.aspx).

You also can own foreign real estate without any reporting requirements. If the IRS or another part of the government ever wanted to seize your foreign bank account, assuming you can even keep it under the new law, it wouldn't be very hard. But they can't seize foreign real estate and bring it back to the States.

Finally, you can own an offshore business. Plenty of people with consulting businesses, import-export or other small businesses set up shop in Panama, and only pay U.S. taxes on the money that business pays them. The rest stays in Panama to compound tax-free, protected by strict bank privacy laws. Of course, when it comes to legal and accounting help in a foreign country, those woods are full of snakes, and you'll want an introduction and references that you actually check.

Watch for a law forbidding U.S. citizens from owning foreign currencies or foreign assets to mark the last desperate attempt to save the U.S. dollar.

CHAPTER 12

Assembling Your Bernanke Portfolio

An ounce of prevention is worth a pound of cure.
—Benjamin Franklin

It is time to assemble your Bernanke Portfolio that will let you and your family survive the Great Inflation, and even a hyperinflation if it comes. I used the word "assemble" instead of "construct" because you just need to take the information in the prior 11 chapters and put it together. This is a long way from rocket science, it is more like assembling a bookshelf from Ikea. But you actually have to do it to get the benefits.

First, the ground rules. You want to avoid the U.S. dollar as much as possible. Cash is trash in an inflation. You want to trade dollars for real assets. You can leverage some or all of these assets with low fixed-rate debt to the extent you can always make the payments, no matter what. At this point in the cycle, avoid adjustable-rate debt at all costs.

Avoid long-term bonds – they are certificates of confiscation of the buying power of your principal. There are some shorter-term, high-yield bonds that make sense, but these "junk" bonds that will pay off are few and far between. It is shocking to me that some financial planners today are telling people to put a third of their portfolios into U.S. Treasury bonds, when we are at the peak of a 28-year bull market in Treasurys. I guess I am easily shocked, but that advice seems similar to me to telling people to buy Webvan or Pets.com at the height of the Internet craze. The idea that retirees should have *any* money in long-term governments is nuts.

The same is true of TIPS, which may protect you against inflation, but not against interest rate risk. Just like any other bond, when the general level of interest rates rises, TIPS prices are hurt because, like regular Treasurys, their percentage interest rate is fixed. In an inflation, and especially in a hyperinflation, market participants will raise the general level of rates to reflect increased uncertainty. That will hurt TIPS substantially. But 2009 was the biggest year for TIPS sales yet, as they hit $18 billion in spite of 1% interest rates. People are buying them just for the inflation protection on the coupon payment, forgetting the hit they could take to the purchasing power of their principal.

And certainly don't count on Social Security or any fixed retirement pay and to see you through, or even be there at all in terms of any useful purchasing power.

Bank Account

Depending on your personal situation, you need three to 12 months of liquid assets. You can open a bank account in Canada or Australia, keep your money there and write checks as needed. Or you can open an account with Everbank in the U.S., and designate that it will be held in Canadian or Australian dollars. Everbank also offers savings accounts designated in gold. You could open one checking account and one savings account in Canadian dollars, and a second savings account in gold. You can move money back and forth by telephone or over the Internet between them. Any time you want your gold, they'll send it to you.

You also need a bag of junk silver at home to use in case of a crisis. This may be the only "bank account" available when the duck comes down. Store it carefully, as discussed above. The "two safes" idea is especially appropriate if you live in an urban or suburban environment, where some not-so-nice people may be going door-to-door taking food, gold and silver.

Hard Assets

Own real estate financed with fixed-rate debt. In the Great Inflation, the debt will essentially become valueless. In a hyperinflation, you'll be able to pay it off with pocket change. In addition to your own home, there are foreclosures and real-estate owned opportunities in vacation areas, golf course developments and small apartment complexes. Rent them out month-to-month so you can raise rents as inflation accelerates. Don't give any long-term leases.

You should have 10% to 20% of your wealth in gold and silver. At current prices, I would advocate 1/3 in gold and 2/3 in silver, using either the physical metals or the mining stock ETFs. If your portfolio is large enough that 7% of it is a large number, consider the Perth Mint certificates or an overseas private vault to get your gold out of the U.S.

Stocks

You can have a large portion of your wealth in stocks, as long as it is in a barbell portfolio. Most of this – 90% or more for most people

– should be in conservative, high-yield value situations. Exchange-traded funds and Master Limited Partnerships in commodities like oil, gas, land and forest products should do especially well. Income trusts with pricing power, such as royalty trusts with a share of the revenues for oil or natural gas sales, also work.

Stocks of multinational companies that can shift their resources to whatever area of the world is doing well should be OK. I would rather see a technology component here than not (Intel instead of Nestle, for example). Owning stocks in areas of currency strength, like Canada, Brazil and China, gives you an extra bonus when it is time to sell.

A small portion of your stock portfolio should be in situations that can return 10 or 20 times your investment, or allow you to build wealth through a series of sequential trades that return 500% or more. I find investments with this kind of potential in development-stage biotechnology, underfollowed electronics technology, alternative energy technology and junior miners. The junior miners are an especially attractive area because they are working with the wind of precious metals prices in their sails, but they also are an especially dangerous area because it is so hard to be successful (not to mention the number of frauds).

Income

It will be very important to have flexible pricing on your income source – a retailer's markup, month-to-month rental agreements on property you own, personal billing rates. For example, there is a nascent trend for doctors to charge an annual retainer fee for patients, separate from any procedures, drugs or supplies reimbursed by private or public insurance. Reimbursement probably will lag inflation in a big way, with hospitals caught in the middle between staff needing wage increases to keep up, while Blue Cross and Medicare move very slowly to increase reimbursements. The doctor in a private retainer-based practice can simply raise the retainer, or even switch to monthly billing.

I probably should set the price of *New World Investor* at two ounces of silver per month, with only a monthly subscription option available.

PART V
What Our Country Could Do, But Won't

Those who govern, having much business on their
hands, do not generally like to take the trouble of
considering and carrying into execution new projects.
The best public measures are therefore seldom adopted
from previous wisdom, but forced by the occasion.
—Benjamin Franklin

CHAPTER 13

"New Projects" Are Needed

alifornia's financial crisis is the Off-Broadway version of the U.S. financial crisis. The State, and the country – and most of the developed world – is broke. We tried an experiment that assumed politicians could be trusted to manage an economy and a currency in a responsible fashion. We were wrong, and the experiment has failed. It is too late to avoid the reset that is coming, which involves an inflation or hyperinflation to wipe out debt holders, followed by the Greatest Depression to wipe out the asset holders. Only when all the debt is liquidated and the assets redistributed to people who can best make use of them will this be behind us.

That process can happen in one of three ways. A government can stay hands-off, let the unwinding happen and get through it. Many people think that is what should have happened. The second way this can play out is to have the government fight the deflation with everything it's got, like patching a dam on the fly as the water gets deeper and deeper behind it, until finally the dam breaks and there is a devastating crash. That is the path Bernanke has put us on.

The third way is to let the process play out over a much longer period of time, trading the speed of the devastating crash for a prolonged period of adjustment. The advantage of this is that the citizens can adapt and spread the pain over a longer period of time. The disadvantage is that it requires a moral compass in Washington that has been lacking for a long time, and a willingness to take on The Powers That Be who support the current political system with their campaign contributions. In other words, the third way is not the most likely outcome.

Here is an example of the third way. About every 15 years, Citicorp, Wells Fargo and Bank of America bring themselves to the brink of failure by leveraging up dumb loans in some popular sector. From Latin America to oil to real estate (twice), they do it again and again as managements try to goose short-term profits to curry favor with Wall Street and increase their personal bonuses.

Each time, the government says they are too big to fail, and the taxpayer bails them out. But while the bank may be too big to fail in the sense of disappearing with the depositors' money, it is the bank holding company that gets bailed out. Why? The holding company has just shown it is too big to succeed, or too dumb to succeed, take your pick.

When Norway's banks got in trouble, they nationalized them. The shareholders and bondholders were wiped out, as they deserved. The upper management was fired, without benefit of golden parachutes granted by their friends on the Boards of Directors, as they deserved. The Boards of Directors were fired, as they deserved. All the bad loans were isolated in "bad banks." Real estate and financial consultants were hired to identify, manage and sell these loans over time to minimize the cost to the taxpayer. The "bad banks" were liquidated. The good banks were taken public again. It's an excellent model for the U.S.

The trouble with applying this "third way" thinking to the whole U.S. economy lies with the voters. Politicians who just voted for a huge budget deficit will say whatever the voter wants to hear. Raise the minimum wage! Subsidize childcare! Start a single-payer healthcare system! Rebuild the bridges and roads! Free computers for the poor! Increase the food stamp program! Subsidize mortgages! Subsidize rents! Re-elect me, and I will be all things to all people!

Bail out the states!

I left California a couple of years ago, when the writing was on the wall for both business taxes and the state budget catastrophe. They can easily balance the budget – just free all 168,000 prison inmates and permanently close all 240 university and community college campuses. The alternative horror shows are not much better – with a bloated budget of $125 billion a year, they'll have a $19 billion deficit in 2010 and a whopping $37 billion in 2011. Will the Federal government bail them out? How about the other 48 states in deep doo-doo, that collectively face shortfalls totaling nearly $300 billion in 2010 and 2011? Not to mention their hundreds of billions more in unfunded pension obligations to their workers? The states will be competing with the Federal government to raise taxes and fees on your income and your assets for years. (See chart next page)

Billionaire Warren Buffett said recently that a Washington bailout of California and other troubled states is inevitable. How, he wondered, can Washington deny California after saying yes to General Motors, AIG and dozens of banks? "I don't know how

Red ink, from sea to shining sea

Forty-eight of 50 states face budget shortfalls this year. Many shortfalls amount to more than 20 per cent of planned spending. The plunge in state tax revenue is the worst on record.

BUDGET SHORTFALLS AS SHARE OF 2010 GENERAL FUND EXPENDITURES
20% and above   Less than 20%   No shortfall

CHANGE IN STATE TAX REVENUE

KATHRYN TAM/THE GLOBE AND MAIL ⋇ SOURCES: U.S. CENSUS BUREAU; CENTER ON BUDGET AND POLICY PRIORITIES

you would tell a state you're going to stiff-arm them with all the bailouts of corporations," Mr. Buffett said. The alternative for many state and local governments may be default. Mr. Buffett said many state and municipal bonds are only triple-A rated because investors assume there's a Federal backstop.

But wait – the Federal government is broke. How are we going to pay for the politicians' promises and the state bailouts?

I know – Raise taxes on the wealthy! (And then pretend that doesn't make it much harder for people and their children to *get* wealthy.)

Oh, wait – even a 100% tax on the wealthy still wouldn't eliminate the budget deficit. So

PRINT MONEY!

The most casual glance at our country's finances show that the government's current fiscal, monetary, and social policies have been an unmitigated disaster. I don't have much hope that they will voluntarily change. Change will be forced on them, and I only hope it doesn't come in the form of a General elected President who decides to suspend elections and rule "for the good of the country."

I think we have to look in the mirror, be honest about what we see, and make a dramatic change in our economic policies, the way we fund politics and the expectations we give to people. We had a beautiful republic, the land of opportunity, a free country that was a beacon to the world. Through a lot of bad choices, we have a near-bankrupt, very militarized, increasingly socialized empire that serves The Powers That Be while trampling the middle class and the Constitution.

I want my country back, for me and my kids. I'm not willing to trade my freedoms for their version of security. Here's how we can get going.

First, Avoid The Wrong Path

If you ask the International Monetary Fund (IMF) how to shrink a budget shortfall, they will tell you to raise taxes and cut spending. The resulting recession will increase the budget shortfall, of course. So if you ask them what to do now, they will tell you to raise taxes further and cut spending farther. The recession will slide into a depression, tax receipts will plunge as private economic activity falters with no offset from increased public activity, and the budget shortfall will get REALLY big. In most countries the

IMF destroys, that is followed by a revolution that throws the incumbents out, puts the IMF folks on a plane home, and dramatically devalues the currency. While the devaluation drives exports to rebuild the economy, the IMF guys write up their notes and declare another victory.

Thus it was with some amusement that I saw the IMF wants the U.S. to cut spending and raise taxes. They even know the specific tax changes they want, starting with getting rid of the home mortgage interest deduction, raising taxes on energy and imposing a national sales tax. Apparently, no one has told them that housing is already a tad weak here, and getting rid of the mortgage interest deduction would bring housing prices down another 20% or so overnight. Or that consumer spending also is weak, so this might not be exactly the right time to lard on a big national sales tax that would kill spending. Not to mention a good-sized energy tax boost to hit the consumer in an area most people can't cut back any further, in a big country that averages a lot of miles per year.

They advised these remarkable policies after saying that the risks to the U.S. economy remain on the downside, including a double-dip recession in housing, continued deterioration in commercial real estate and pressures on exports due to the European debt crises. They must have one group that defines the risks and a second group that comes up with the policies, and they don't talk to each other. Either that, or the policy group thought someone asked them what were the *worst* things President Obama could do, given the risks.

A U.S. official with tongue firmly in cheek said that the IMF had used forecasts for economic growth and interest rates that were too pessimistic compared to the consensus of most private forecasters and this had the impact of inflating the government's deficit problem over the next decade. He forgot to add that it also had the impact of inflating the need for the IMF to say anything at all, or pretend to be relevant.

Second, Brainstorm The Right Path

In the spirit of "in the Kingdom of the Blind, the one-eyed is king" I thought I would lay out what I would like to see the Administration do to get out of this mess quickly. In other words, with idiots like these giving advice, why shouldn't a person of at least average intelligence like myself give better advice? I have a T-shirt that says: "I am not smart, but I can lift heavy things." Those wussies can't lift anything heavier than their cell phones and lattes. Maybe they will read the next chapter.

CHAPTER 14

An Open Letter to President Obama

 ear Mr. President:

As I'm sure you have realized by now, you are pretty much screwed. A series of Presidents and Congresses before you made many bad decisions that periodically got the economy into a mess. I am non-partisan about this; the last President with both integrity and fiscal sense was Dwight Eisenhower. It's been a long time building. Even with the string of losers that have run this country since Ike, there have been some tough-minded Fed Chairman that kept some limits on the chaos. But that ended with Paul Volker, and since he left, every mess has been monetized by the Fed and the can kicked down the road. So now the can is at the end of the road, the messes have gotten so large that everyone knows the next one is the tsunami, and your approval ratings are in the toilet with, at this writing, mid-term elections coming up.

You had a chance to blame everything on George W., stop the stupid trickle-down bailouts that just turned into eye-popping bonuses for the morons who got us into this (they should all go work for the IMF), and use some dramatic policy changes to give people – what was it? Oh, yeah. Change and hope. But you didn't do it. Had your chance. Muffed it.

Or did you? Starting today (and you had better get started today) you have very little time before the election. Here is what you can and must do to (a) save the country, (b) save your party on November 2, and (c) save your reputation – indeed, turn it from ineffective goat (sorry – tough love, there) to crusading hero for *C*H*A*N*G*E*!!!

1. You are surrounded by Wall Street and establishment hacks from the Clinton era. Get rid of them. Summers did you a great favor by resigning. Fire Bernanke and Geithner immediately. If you are listening to Robert Rubin in any way, stop it. Or appoint him to something, just so you can fire him. That's because in the great tradition of CEOs everywhere, you need them to be the goat, not you. Blame the failed policies of these guys you fired plus Hank Paulson and George W. Bush for getting us to where we are today. If anyone asks any embarrassing questions, say you were misled.

2. You are going to make four major moves to turn this situation around 180^0. Please sit down as you read this; I would not want you to get hurt if you faint. The first is a fiscal move. You are going to rebate all individual income taxes paid for the last three years, with a minimum check of $25,000 to single taxpayers and $50,000 to those filing jointly. Yes, if they filed jointly and paid $2,000 in taxes over the last three years they get $50,000 back. If they paid $50,000, they get $50,000 back. If they paid $250,000, they get it all back. What if they had such a low income they didn't even file? They still get $25,000 or $50,000 back. It's trickle-*up,* and it will work.

I want you to be very Presidential about this. Go on TV and urge people to take this as a do-over to get rid of their credit card debt, get caught up on their house payments, buy snow tires or do some elective surgery. You might have Billy Graham talk about the Jubilee Year, if he is still alive. Urge the community do-gooder organizations to put programs in place to advise people on how not to blow their one-time windfall.

Nancy Pelosi will be mad as hell. Harry Reid won't be – he is in danger of getting whipped in November if you don't do something popular. Just point out to Nancy that those paying over $250,000 paid about 80% of the taxes for the last three years, but are only getting 5% of the money flowing back. I am making those numbers up, but you get my drift.

Won't this cause inflation to take off? Not right away – we have too much unused capacity, and the Chinese have too much stuff in warehouses that they have been churning out to keep their pretend GDP numbers up, with no buyers. Believe me, GM will not run out of Silverados just because all the tattooed 20-somethings get an unexpected $25,000 in the mail. But they will sell a hell of a lot of Silverados. Later, inflation is going to skyrocket anyway, and you can (correctly) blame it on Bernanke, Geithner, Summers, Paulson and Bush. (And Rubin, if you can find him. He seems to have disappeared. No need to mention Greenspan; everyone has figured out that he started it.)

Won't this cause the dollar to tank against the other currencies, gold and silver? Yes. But the dollar is a Dead Man Walking. The Fed has destroyed 94% of the dollar's value since 1913. This will destroy the remaining 6% by 2013, but not to worry – you are going to blame it on Bernanke *et. al.*, remember? And that brings us to your second major move.

3. You are going to leave the Federal Reserve Board as the supervisor of banks, but take away their ability to create money and credit and give it back to the Treasury Department. You have some convenient cover for this: It is what the Constitution called

for in Article I, Section 8, Clause 5, because as Thomas Jefferson famously said: "If the American people ever allow private banks to control the issuance of their currency, first by inflation and then by deflation, the banks and corporations that will grow up around them will deprive the people of all their property until their children will wake up homeless on the continent their fathers conquered."

Is that prescient, stirring stuff, or what? You can look straight at the teleprompter and read that, and you'll have Glenn Beck shouting: "Hallelujah!" Well, maybe not Glenn Beck, but pretty much everyone else.

The cool part is that when the Fed was established, there was a backout clause that let the government buy them out for $1 billion. It must have seemed like a huge amount of money to the banksters that secretly created the Fed. Today, not so much.

One warning: President Kennedy decided to end the Federal Reserve System and issued an Executive Order that the U.S. government was to reclaim its Constitutional mandate to control the money. Three weeks later, he was dead, and Lyndon Johnson vacated the order. Watch your back; like the naked shortsellers, the banksters can play rough.

4. Okay, only two to go. Your third move is to let Federal Reserve Notes die of their own weight by issuing only Treasury Notes in the future that are 100% backed by gold. You'll have to revalue gold to about $20,000 an ounce, and stand ready to buy gold at that price with Treasury Notes or sell gold at that price for Treasury Notes. You will not accept Federal Reserve Notes for gold. Federal Reserve Notes can still circulate for anyone who wants to use them, with the conversion ratio between FRNs and TNs set by the market. Believe me, FR notes will disappear in a hurry – an example of good money driving out bad. A gold-backed Treasury dollar will be the world's reserve currency for the next 100 years.

Now, what does revaluing gold to $20,000 an ounce do? It makes those who hold gold much, much richer. And who holds the most gold? You do! It's in Fort Knox and the vaults of the New York Fed, which is holding it for you. Incidentally, I would get it out of the NYFed – be sure you count it – and move it back to Fort Knox. Also, run a physical audit on Fort Knox, would you? People talk. Just being careful. But the U.S. government holds more gold than pretty much anybody, and if you are willing to pay $20,000 an ounce in crispy new Treasury Notes 100% backed by gold for more of it, then by golly you might even find some sellers to add to the hoard.

As a thought, the U.S. debt that was issued while the Federal Reserve was issuing notes could be paid off only in FRNs. Depends how mean you want to be to China, Japan and Russia. Remember that those guys hold a heck of a lot of gold, too, so you will be doing them a huge favor by revaluing gold to $20,000 an ounce. They will be able to afford a haircut on the debt repayment.

5. This is it – your fourth and last move, and it is the lulu that gives you a sweep in November and a second term. It also saves the whole country, but I know that is a lesser priority than a sweep in November and a second term.

You are going to abolish all personal and corporate income taxes, and Social Security and Medicare taxes, and urge the states to abolish their income taxes. Completely abolish them. Give reasonable severance to the civil servants of the IRS, of course, who can then find productive work that does not involve robbing their fellow citizens on a daily basis.

You are going to replace the income and FICA taxes with the Fair Tax. Please see FairTax.org. The Fair Tax is a national sales tax with an up-front rebate to take care of low-income folks. You see, Mr. President, if you want less of something, like cigarette smoking (sorry, couldn't resist), you raise taxes on it. We want *more* income in this country, not less. More income means more jobs, more savings and more investment. We want *less* consumption to get our trade deficit down, and also to get people off the treadmill of keeping up with the Joneses by using their credit cards. So we tax consumption, not income. Get it?

This makes the expiring Bush tax cuts a non-issue. And don't even think about piling a VAT tax or a sales tax on top of the income tax, because that would just depress the economy and make people mad at you. Now imagine this: You go on TV and tell your loyal subjects that you are not only rebating the last three years of their income taxes in cash, but they will never again have to pay income taxes and you will personally work to repeal the 16th Amendment. The Republicans won't even run against you in 2012! Or maybe they'll put up Glenn Beck and Rush Limbaugh as sacrificial lambs – big sacrificial lambs, so to speak.

These four steps are all you have to do to get us out of the mess, unleash American ingenuity into a flood of new economic growth (the only real way out of this mess) and be the hero you know you deserve to be. (That's coaching language.)

- A huge tax rebate to jump-start the economy for real this time
- Get rid of the Fed and their Federal Reserve Notes
- Go back to honest money
- Get rid of the IRS and substitute consumption-based tax revenue

But if you want a bonus, here's a fifth idea: Have a one-time tax holiday with no criminal prosecutions for those who have stashed money overseas, either in tax shelters or just illegal cash accounts. They can bring it back to the U.S. and pay only 10% taxes, no questions asked. The rich and the thugs – am I being redundant? – with semi-legal or illegal money overseas will bring it back, liquefy our banks and pay you a bolus of cash when you could use it. As I said, it's a bonus idea.

I have a few others for your second term: Legalize most recreational drugs, tax them and allow them to be distributed through the existing system so you can keep track of who's using them too much, and get them some help. The subsequent collapse in the Mexican, Columbian and Afghanistan economies is not our problem. The savings in prison costs and being able to recapture the inner cities is our gain.

Speaking of Afghanistan, get out of there right away. Cut a deal with the Taliban: We'll stop supporting the corrupt Karzais if the Taliban will guarantee women's rights, religious freedom and unrestricted Internet access when they take power. If they break their word after a while, let the Afghani people punish them. It's not our job. After we're out of Afghanistan, go to Iraq, declare victory and get out of there, too. That's not our job, either. Never was.

After you save $1 trillion by extricating us from those two wars, let's talk about banning high fructose corn syrup to reverse the obesity problem, getting rid of the ethanol boondoggle and import tax, and taking another look at the long-term effects of genetically modified seeds, fluoride in the water supply and confined animal feeding operations. Also regulatory capture of the SEC and FDA. That ought to be enough to get you to 2016 as the greatest President in 50 years.

Regards,

Michael Murphy CFA, Editor
New World Investor

P.S. As for Social Security and Medicare, the new high economic growth will solve the problem. Just appoint a commission and kick that can down the road.

CHAPTER 15

The Fair Tax: Not Flat, Not VAT, Just Simple and Practical

Democracy is two wolves and a lamb voting on what to have for lunch. Liberty is a well-armed lamb contesting the vote.
—Benjamin Franklin

Federal taxes are one area of our economy that requires radical restructuring. As long as the voters put up with the IRS, politicians stirring up class warfare for votes, and a tax code that is so hopelessly complex even IRS consultants can't agree on what it says, this country is going nowhere. Productive people and entrepreneurs are being squeezed by the same mindless, python-like government forces that have turned most of Europe into an uncompetitive museum.

In my newsletter, I frequently mentioned my enthusiasm for replacing the personal and corporate income tax with a value-added tax (VAT) that includes an exemption for rent and unprocessed food, to lighten the load on lower-income households. *New World Investor* subscriber Helen A. emailed me: "Is there a reason why you recommend a VAT tax on everything other than rent and unprocessed food over the Fair Tax? If you aren't familiar with the Fair Tax, I would be delighted to send you a couple of books about it. Incidentally, my engineering consulting firm has an easier time getting international contracts because our European competition needs to add VAT to their consulting rates."

So I spent several days reading about the Fair Tax and emailed her back: "Yes, there is a reason I recommended the VAT – ignorance. The Fair Tax is a much better solution."

It is a shibboleth in economics that if you want less of something, tax it. Raise the taxes on cigarettes and fewer people will smoke. Raise the taxes on liquor and fewer people will drink. Raise the taxes on income and fewer people will work harder – wait a minute! Raise the business taxes on employing people and fewer jobs will be created – now hold on!

If Congress understood this very basic economic relationship, I wonder how different our taxation system would look. The income tax needs to be ripped out by the roots, but the original taxes our country relied on to fund the Federal government – import taxes – are pretty much illegal under various trade treaties. (Although I think some of those should be re-imposed on countries china that are not china playing by china the rules china.)

Thus the search by some economists and politicians, not to mention lay people who realize the current tax system is a crock, for an alternative. There are three on the table: the Flat Tax, in which the idea of an income tax survives but a flat percentage is applied to everyone; the VAT, in which taxes are collected by the manufacturer s at each stage of production; and the Fair Tax, which is a national sales tax on the sale of all new goods and services. All three are better than the current income tax system, but the Fair Tax is the best alternative. Here's why.

The Flat Tax

The flat tax, or flat rate tax, is a simple proposal to tax all business and personal income one time at a fixed rate, say 20%. Proponents say that the tax return is reduced to a postcard with 10 lines. There is a fixed exemption for every business and personal filer; say, $10,000 a year, in order to avoid burdening low-income taxpayers. A married couple filing jointly would have two exemptions, or $20,000 a year. There would be no double taxation, or taxation of a return on money on which taxes were already paid. So capital gains, dividends, interest and estate taxes would go away.

Obviously, by fiddling with the rate and the fixed exemption, the flat tax can be made revenue-neutral to the government. It would neither increase nor decrease the deficit – that depends on spending decisions. The advantages of the flat tax include the simpler tax structure and the removal of progressively higher rate brackets that discourage people from working harder. Many people don't realize that there is a remarkable turnover during any five year period of who is in the top 20% and bottom 20% brackets. Policies designed to "soak the rich" turns out to also "soak those who are trying to get rich." In the very top brackets, taxpayers can afford professional legal and accounting advice to find loopholes and structures that will reduce their taxes, so these "soak those who are trying to get rich" policies tend to fall hardest on those making the great American intra-class jump, from lower middle-class to upper middle-class.

Proponents of the flat tax point out that is costs about $265 billion to collect taxes, including enforcement. The current Revenue Code is over nine million words long with numerous loopholes, deductions, and exemptions. If you ask 50 tax preparers or IRS employees to fill out a hypothetical return, you will get

40 to 45 different tax amounts. If you call the IRS with a complex question, even the IRS admits you will get a wrong answer 20% to 33% of the time.

The *Economist* claims that such a flat tax would reduce the number of entities required to file returns from about 130 million individuals, households, and businesses at present to a mere eight million businesses and self-employed. Actually, even with companies withholding and paying the flat tax on their employees' compensation to the government, I think everyone would at least have to file the postcard.

Some worry about the effect of a flat tax on charitable contributions and housing, as those deductions go away. During the 1980s, the top tax rate was reduced dramatically from 70% to 28%. The value of housing did not drop, and charitable contributions rose sharply during the '80s as the economy improved. Others worry that a future Administration could simply raise the flat tax. Until we have a Constitutional amendment to require a super-majority to raise the flat tax rate, they could. But it would be in the glare of publicity, instead of buried in a 2,000-page bill that no one has read, and might be terminal to the career of any politician who voted for it.

What's wrong with the flat tax? Two big things. First, it does not get rid of the IRS. Second, the complexity in our tax code does not come from the progressive rate structure. That is a one- or two-page lookup or simple calculation. The complexity comes from defining "income" and all the rules created over the years on what is an expense and what is not, the various types of depreciation, the timing issues of when income is received, and so on. For example, employee club dues are not currently deductible as a business expense. Travel and entertainment expenses are only

50% deductible. Neither of those rules would change under the flat tax, so companies would still have to have bookkeepers to keep track of them and accountants to review them. The IRS would still have to have auditors to audit them, and their whole process of challenges, audits, late fees and penalties would be intact.

A country could have a simple tax code with a progressive rate structure, or a complex tax code like the U.S. with a flat rate structure. Eastern Europe, Russia and Hong Kong are all examples of the latter. Russia shocked the world when they adopted a 13% flat tax, and it has worked wonders for their economy. But I want to see a simple tax code *AND* a flat rate structure, so I gave up on the flat tax.

The VAT Tax

The value-added tax or VAT works this way: At each stage of production, a company pays a tax on its purchases. When it sells an item, it charges a tax. It then subtracts the tax it paid from the tax it collected, and sends the difference to the government. For example, say a miner sells a pound of smelted copper for $2, and there is a 20% VAT. The miner sends 40 cents to the government. The buyer of the copper turns it into copper wire and sells it for $8. They collect $1.60 in VAT, credit themselves for the 40 cents of VAT they paid to the miner, and send $1.20 to the government.

The buyer of the copper wire manufactures headphones, which they sell to a distributor for $40. They collect $8 in VAT, subtract the $1.60 they paid in VAT, and send $6.40 to the government. The distributor sells the headphones to Radio Shack for $50, collects $10 in VAT, subtracts the $8 VAT they paid, and send $2 to the government. Radio Shack sells the headphones to you for

$100, collects $20 in VAT, subtracts the $10 they paid, and sends $10 to the government.

Ultimately, you paid $20 in VAT to buy a $100 pair of head-phones. The government got 40 cents from the miner, $1.20 from the wire manufacturer, $6.40 from the headphone manufacturer, $2 from the distributor and $10 from Radio Shack. $0.40 + $1.20 + $6.40 + $2 + $10 = $20.00.

One advantage of VAT is that it is self-policing. The headphone manufacturer, for example, will report that they paid $1.60 in VAT to the wire manufacturer. If the wire manufacturer fails to report that and tries to keep it, the government will know.

But there are two disadvantages to VAT. One is that it is need-lessly complex. You paid $20 to Radio Shack. Why not just call that a sales tax and have Radio Shack send it to the government? There's a lot of pointless record-keeping along the way to collect the same amount of money. It is true that Europe introduced the VAT because high sales taxes caused cheating and smuggling. But that was in an era and place of small retailers. In the U.S., 80% of retail sales are through national chains that are unlikely to under-report a sales tax.

The other problem with a VAT is that governments want to impose it *in addition to* the income tax. The Obama Administra-tion is studying this alternative right now, and we have the example of Europe as a slow-growth, over-taxed area with both a high VAT and a high, progressive tax on income. It is really crucial that the 16th Amendment, which allows for a tax on income, be repealed before either a VAT or a national sales tax is implemented. Fortu-nately, if the Obama Administration introduces legislation for a VAT at a low level, probably 3% or so, that bill can become a vehicle for a 23% national sales tax accompanied by an abolition of the income tax. Which brings us to...

The Fair Tax

From the FairTax.org website:

The FairTax plan is a comprehensive proposal that replaces all federal income and payroll based taxes with an integrated approach including a progressive national retail sales tax, a "prebate" to ensure no American pays federal taxes on spending up to the poverty level, dollar-for-dollar federal revenue neutrality, and, through companion legislation, the repeal of the 16th Amendment.

The FairTax Act (HR 25, S 296) is nonpartisan legislation. It abolishes all federal personal and corporate income taxes, gift, estate, capital gains, alternative minimum, Social Security, Medicare, and self-employment taxes and replaces them with one simple, visible, federal retail sales tax administered primarily by existing state sales tax authorities.

The FairTax taxes us only on what we choose to spend on new goods or services, not on what we earn. The FairTax is a fair, efficient, transparent, and intelligent solution to the frustration and inequity of our current tax system.

The FairTax:

- Enables workers to keep their entire paychecks
- Enables retirees to keep their entire pensions
- Refunds in advance the tax on purchases of basic necessities
- Allows American products to compete fairly
- Brings transparency and accountability to tax policy
- Ensures Social Security and Medicare funding
- Closes all loopholes and brings fairness to taxation
- Abolishes the IRS

* * * * *

The Fair Tax is a national sales tax, imposed only at the retail level. All business-to-business transactions are exempt, and all retail transactions are taxed, including purchases over the Internet. Like the flat tax, it is a single rate and is not imposed on money that has been taxed before, so capital gains, interest income, dividends and estates are tax-free. It also is set high enough to cover Social Security and Medicare taxes, and be revenue-neutral to the current tax code.

The Fair Tax appeals to me because it taxes consumption, not income. If we are ever going to get out of this mess, we need Americans to work hard, generate lots of income, save more to fund investment, and reduce their consumption, especially the over-consumption based on taking on debt. The Fair Tax encourages the things we want and discourages the things we don't want. It is extremely easy to collect because 45 states already have sales taxes, and the Fair Tax can be piggybacked onto that structure. As written, the Fair Tax Bill includes a 0.25% credit to the retailers collecting the tax, and another 0.25% credit to the states processing the collections and forwarding the Federal government its share.

In order to avoid overburdening the chronic or temporary poor, the Fair Tax includes a "prebate." The government has calculated the poverty level of income for families of different sizes:

2009 FairTax Prebate Schedule[1]							
One adult household				Two adult household			
Family Size	Annual Consumption Allowance	Annual Rebate	Monthly Rebate	Family Size	Annual Consumption Allowance	Annual Rebate	Monthly Rebate
1 person	$10,830	$2,491	$208	couple	$21,660	$4,982	$415
and 1 child	$14,570	$3,351	$279	and 1 child	$25,400	$5,842	$487
and 2 children	$18,310	$4,211	$351	and 2 children	$29,140	$6,702	$559
and 3 children	$22,050	$5,072	$423	and 3 children	$32,880	$7,562	$630
and 4 children	$25,790	$5,932	$494	and 4 children	$36,620	$8,423	$702
and 5 children	$29,530	$6,792	$566	and 5 children	$40,360	$9,283	$774
and 6 children	$32,270	$7,422	$619	and 6 children	$44,100	$10,143	$845
and 7 children	$37,010	$8,512	$709	and 7 children	$47,840	$11,003	$917

[1]SOURCE: The ACA is based on the 2009 DHHS Poverty Guidelines published in the Federal Register, Vol. 74 No. 14, January 23, 2009, pp. 4199-4201

The "prebate" is simply a transfer payment from the government that will cover the Fair Tax on consumption at the poverty level, given family size. Everyone gets the prebate, no matter what their income. This does not make the Fair Tax "progressive" – it simply means that no one has to pay a consumption tax on spending up to the poverty level. They have calculated that a 23% rate will cover the prebate, Social Security and Medicare, and completely replace the current revenues from corporate and individual income taxes.

Incidentally, the 23% rate they are proposing is an "inclusive" rate, like the current income tax. Example: Someone makes $125 and pays $25 in taxes, so their tax rate is 20% on the base that includes the tax. On an "exclusive" basis we would say that the person took home $100 and the government took $25, which is 25% of their take-home pay. Sales taxes are usually calculated on an "exclusive" basis, and on that basis the real Fair Tax rate is 29.9%. They are using the lower 23% inclusive rate just for public relations purposes, to make it comparable to the quoted income tax rates.

There have been two government studies (the Joint Committee on Taxation and the President's Advisory Panel on Federal Tax Reform) that claim that the tax rate of the Fair Tax bill, 29.9% on a tax-exclusive basis, is approximately one-half of the rate necessary to be revenue-neutral. That is nonsense. Neither study takes the Fair Tax Bill as written and analyzes it. Each study made a number of assumptions about why this or that provision would have to be changed, and then after the change – *voila!* – the Fair Tax rate is too low. Hogwash. If the Federal government really needed 58.8% of all the consumption in the United States to replace its current tax revenues, we would be in much worse shape than Europe. Add another 11% or so for the average state sales tax and income tax, and these studies are claiming that government at every level needs about 70% of consumption to survive. That is ridiculous.

It is pretty appalling to think that we have to have even a 30% sales tax just to fund the Federal government, plus another 5% to 10% to fund state and local governments. Perhaps these rates will eventually cause voters to insist that government at every level get their spending under control. Individually, people will have the ability to control how much they pay in taxes by controlling their own spending. Money saved is money not taxed, nor will the interest, dividends or capital gains on it be taxed. Money saved becomes money available for investment in our economy.

If we can get a national sales tax to replace the income tax, I expect virtually every state would fall in line quickly. It simply costs too much to collect an income tax, and without the IRS to piggyback on, it isn't practical. The states can raise their sales taxes to the level they need to be revenue-neutral and be done with it. When New Yorkers discover they need a 20% state sales tax, maybe even they will revolt against the waste and fraud in their system.

Do we still need the IRS?

Although the symbolism of getting completely rid of the IRS is wonderful, the truth is that under either a VAT or the Fair Tax, there are ways to cheat and a policeman is needed. The advantage is that instead of millions of potential targets for the revenue police to monitor, enforcement can focus on a much smaller number of entities. A general economic idea is that if sales taxes exceed 10%, people start engaging in tax-evading activity. Cheating, mainly by pretending to be a business, buying at wholesale, or buying products through an employer will exist. Our experience with high cigarette taxes is proof that smuggling could be a problem.

This is one area where the VAT has an advantage. VAT rates can rise above 10% without widespread evasion because of the novel collection mechanism. However, because of its particular mechanism of collection, VAT quite easily becomes the target of specific frauds, which can be very expensive in terms of loss of tax incomes for states.

The bottom line is that some people will try to cheat, whether we have a flat tax, VAT or Fair Tax, and we still need a policeman. It shouldn't be named Internal Revenue Service because that is an institution and era that we need to put behind us. Maybe the Fair Tax Office?

Afterword

They who can give up essential liberty to obtain a little temporary safety deserve neither liberty nor safety.

—Benjamin Franklin

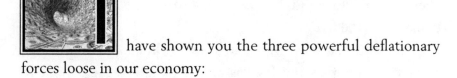 have shown you the three powerful deflationary forces loose in our economy:

- The Demographics of aging baby boomers
- The Generational Economics of the shift to Millennials and GenX
- The impact of Technology Everywhere

I've also shown you that Fed Chairman Bernanke doesn't see Demographics or Technology at all, and thinks Generational Economics is only a credit implosion problem that he can solve by printing money and creating credit by taking on debt. He has the power and motivation to drive down the value of the dollar to reduce the real burden of all the new debt, and he is following policies that are having that effect.

So you need to protect yourself from the coming Great Inflation, which may spiral out of control into a disastrous hyperinflation.

You will get out of dollars, and you won't hold bonds. You will buy real assets – real estate, precious metals, commodities, stocks – and perhaps judiciously leverage them with fixed-rate debt you can afford. You will keep at least some of your junk silver and a little gold where you can get your hands on it in an emergency.

Your stock portfolio will follow the barbell model, with most of it in safe, high-yield investments that will steadily compound your wealth, and a small part of it in swing-for-the-fences situations that can dramatically change your economic situation if the work out. You won't hold the mass of popular institutional stocks in the middle, where returns tend to be low, volatility high as the proprietary trading desks play their games, and risks hard to quantify.

Most important, you will actually do these things NOW while they are on your mind, because "tomorrow" is when the shift is going to hit the fan.

And if you have the time and are so inclined, please sit down with your relatives and friends and tell them what's about to happen. If a politician asks you for your vote, ask them some hard questions about the issues you've just educated yourself on. And especially push, push, push for the Fair Tax. We are never going to get this big ship turned in a better direction if they can take all the money they want from us and spend it to benefit their biggest contributors. That game has to end if we are going to get our America back.

APPENDIX A

Deflation: Making Sure "It" Doesn't Happen Here

Remarks by Governor Ben S. Bernanke
Before the National Economists Club, Washington, D.C.
November 21, 2002

Since World War II, inflation – the apparently inexorable rise in the prices of goods and services – has been the bane of central bankers. Economists of various stripes have argued that inflation is the inevitable result of (pick your favorite) the abandonment of metallic monetary standards, a lack of fiscal discipline, shocks to the price of oil and other commodities, struggles over the distribution of income, excessive money creation, self-confirming inflation expectations, an "inflation bias" in the policies of central banks, and still others. Despite widespread "inflation pessimism," however, during the 1980s and 1990s most industrial-country central banks were able to cage, if not entirely tame, the inflation dragon. Although a number of factors converged to make this happy outcome possible, an essential element was the heightened understanding by central bankers and, equally as important, by political leaders and the public at large of the very high costs of allowing the economy to stray too far from price stability.

With inflation rates now quite low in the United States, however, some have expressed concern that we may soon face a new problem – the danger of deflation, or falling prices. That this concern is not purely hypothetical is brought home to us whenever we read newspaper reports about Japan, where what seems to be a relatively moderate *deflation* – a decline in consumer prices of about 1 percent per year – has been associated with years of painfully slow growth, rising joblessness, and apparently intractable financial problems in the banking and corporate sectors. While it is difficult to sort out cause from effect, the consensus view is that deflation has been an important negative factor in the Japanese slump.

So, is deflation a threat to the economic health of the United States? Not to leave you in suspense, I believe that the chance of significant deflation in the United States in the foreseeable future is extremely small, for two principal reasons. The first is the resilience and structural stability of the U.S. economy itself. Over the years, the U.S. economy has shown a remarkable ability to absorb shocks of all kinds, to recover, and to continue to grow. Flexible and efficient markets for labor and capital, an entrepreneurial tradition, and a general willingness to tolerate and even embrace technological and economic change all contribute to this resiliency. A particularly important protective factor in the current environment is the strength of our financial system: Despite the adverse shocks of the past year, our banking system remains healthy and well-regulated, and firm and household balance sheets are for the most part in good shape. Also helpful is that inflation has recently been not only low but quite stable, with one result being that inflation expectations seem well anchored. For example, according to the University of Michigan survey that underlies the index of consumer sentiment, the median expected rate of inflation during the next five to ten years among those interviewed was 2.9 percent in October 2002, as compared with 2.7 percent a year earlier and 3.0 percent two years earlier – a stable record indeed.

The second bulwark against deflation in the United States, and the one that will be the focus of my remarks today, is the Federal Reserve System itself. The Congress has given the Fed the responsibility of preserving price stability (among other objectives), which most definitely implies avoiding deflation as well as inflation. I am confident that the Fed would take whatever means necessary to prevent significant deflation in the United States and, moreover, that the U.S. central bank, in cooperation with other parts of the government as needed, has sufficient policy instruments to ensure that any deflation that might occur would be both mild and brief.

Of course, we must take care lest confidence become overconfidence. Deflationary episodes are rare, and generalization about them is difficult. Indeed, a recent Federal Reserve study of the Japanese experience concluded that the deflation there was almost entirely unexpected, by both foreign and Japanese observers alike (Ahearne et al., 2002). So, having said that deflation in the United States is highly unlikely, I would be imprudent to rule out the possibility altogether. Accordingly, I want to turn to a further exploration of the causes of deflation, its economic effects, and the policy instruments that can be deployed against it. Before going further I should say that my comments today reflect my own views only and are not necessarily those of my colleagues on the Board of Governors or the Federal Open Market Committee.

Deflation: Its Causes and Effects

Deflation is defined as a general decline in prices, with emphasis on the word "general." At any given time, especially in a low-inflation economy like that of our recent experience, prices of some goods and services will be falling. Price declines in a specific sector may occur because productivity is rising and costs are falling more quickly in that sector than elsewhere or because the demand for the output of that sector is weak relative to the demand for other goods and services. Sector-specific price declines, uncomfortable as they may be for producers in that sector, are generally not a problem for the economy as a whole and do not constitute deflation. Deflation *per se* occurs only when price declines are so widespread that broad-based indexes of prices, such as the consumer price index, register ongoing declines.

The sources of deflation are not a mystery. Deflation is in almost all cases a side effect of a collapse of aggregate demand – a drop in spending so severe that producers must cut prices on an ongoing basis in order to find buyers.[1] Likewise, the economic effects of a deflationary episode, for the most part, are similar to those of any other sharp decline in aggregate spending – namely, recession, rising unemployment, and financial stress.

However, a deflationary recession may differ in one respect from "normal" recessions in which the inflation rate is at least modestly positive: Deflation of sufficient magnitude may result in the nominal interest rate declining to zero or very close to zero.[2] Once the nominal interest rate is at zero, no further downward adjustment in the rate can occur, since lenders generally will not accept a negative nominal interest rate when it is possible instead to hold cash. At this point, the nominal interest rate is said to have hit the "zero bound."

Deflation great enough to bring the nominal interest rate close to zero poses special problems for the economy and for policy. First, when the nominal interest rate has been reduced to zero, the *real* interest rate paid by borrowers equals the expected rate of deflation, however large that may be.[3] To take what might seem like an extreme example (though in fact it occurred in the United States in the early 1930s), suppose that deflation is proceeding at a clip of 10 percent per year. Then someone who borrows for a year at a nominal interest rate of zero actually faces a 10 percent *real* cost of funds, as the loan must be repaid in dollars whose purchasing power is 10 percent greater than that of the dollars borrowed originally. In a period of sufficiently severe deflation, the real cost of borrowing becomes prohibitive. Capital investment, purchases of new homes, and other types of spending decline accordingly, worsening the economic downturn.

Although deflation and the zero bound on nominal interest rates create a significant problem for those seeking to borrow, they impose an even greater burden on households and firms that had accumulated substantial debt before the onset of the deflation. This burden arises because, even if debtors are able to refinance their existing obligations at low nominal interest rates, with prices falling they must still repay the principal in dollars of increasing (perhaps rapidly increasing) real value. When William Jennings Bryan made his famous "cross of gold" speech in his 1896 presidential campaign, he was speaking on behalf of heavily mortgaged farmers whose debt burdens were growing ever larger in real terms, the result of a sustained deflation that followed America's post-Civil-War return to the gold standard.[4] The financial distress of debtors can, in turn, increase the fragility of the nation's financial system – for example, by leading to a rapid increase in the share of bank loans that are delinquent or in default. Japan in recent years has certainly faced the problem of "debt-deflation" – the deflation-induced, ever-increasing real value of debts. Closer to home, massive financial problems, including defaults, bankruptcies, and bank failures, were endemic in America's worst encounter with deflation, in the years 1930-33 – a period in which (as I mentioned) the U.S. price level fell about 10 percent per year.

Beyond its adverse effects in financial markets and on borrowers, the zero bound on the nominal interest rate raises another concern – the limitation that it places on conventional monetary policy. Under normal conditions, the Fed and most other central banks implement policy by setting a target for a short-term interest rate – the overnight federal funds rate in the United States – and enforcing that target by buying and selling securities in open capital markets. When the short-term interest rate hits zero, the central bank can no longer ease policy by lowering its usual interest-rate target.[5]

Because central banks conventionally conduct monetary policy by manipulating the short-term nominal interest rate, some observers have concluded that when that key rate stands at or near zero, the central bank has "run out of ammunition" – that is, it no longer has the power to expand aggregate demand and hence economic activity. It is true that once the policy rate has been driven down to zero, a central bank can no longer use its *traditional* means of stimulating aggregate demand and thus will be operating in less familiar territory. The central bank's inability to use its traditional methods may complicate the policymaking process and introduce uncertainty in the size and timing of the economy's response to policy actions. Hence I agree that the situation is one to be avoided if possible.

However, a principal message of my talk today is that a central bank whose accustomed policy rate has been forced down to zero has most definitely *not* run out of ammunition. As I will discuss, a central bank, either alone or in cooperation with other parts of the government, retains considerable power to expand aggregate demand and economic activity even when its accustomed policy rate is at zero. In the remainder of my talk, I will first discuss measures for preventing deflation – the preferable option if feasible. I will then turn to policy measures that the Fed and other government authorities can take if prevention efforts fail and deflation appears to be gaining a foothold in the economy.

Preventing Deflation

As I have already emphasized, deflation is generally the result of low and falling aggregate demand. The basic prescription for preventing deflation is therefore straightforward, at least in principle: Use monetary and fiscal policy as needed to support aggregate spending, in a manner as nearly consistent as possible with full utilization of economic resources and low and stable inflation. In other words, the best way to get out of trouble is not to get into it in the first place. Beyond this commonsense injunction, however, there are several measures that the Fed (or any central bank) can take to reduce the risk of falling into deflation.

First, the Fed should try to preserve a buffer zone for the inflation rate, that is, during normal times it should not try to push inflation down all the way to zero.[6] Most central banks seem to understand the need for a buffer zone. For example, central banks with explicit inflation targets almost invariably set their target for inflation above zero, generally between 1 and 3 percent per year. Maintaining an inflation buffer zone reduces the risk that a large, unanticipated drop in aggregate demand will drive the economy far enough into deflationary territory to lower the nominal interest rate to zero. Of course, this benefit of having a buffer zone for inflation must be weighed against the costs associated with allowing a higher inflation rate in normal times.

Second, the Fed should take most seriously – as of course it does – its responsibility to ensure financial stability in the economy. Irving Fisher (1933) was perhaps the first economist to emphasize the potential connections between violent financial crises, which lead to "fire sales" of assets and falling asset prices, with general declines in aggregate demand and the price level. A healthy, well capitalized banking system and smoothly functioning capital markets are an important line of defense against deflationary shocks. The Fed should and does use its regulatory and supervisory powers to ensure that the financial system will remain resilient if financial conditions change rapidly. And at times of extreme threat to financial stability, the Federal Reserve stands ready to use the discount window and other tools to protect the financial system, as it did during the 1987 stock market crash and the September 11, 2001, terrorist attacks.

Third, as suggested by a number of studies, when inflation is already low and the fundamentals of the economy suddenly deteriorate, the central bank should act more preemptively and more aggressively than usual in cutting rates (Orphanides and Wieland, 2000; Reifschneider and Williams, 2000; Ahearne et al., 2002). By moving decisively and early, the Fed may be able to prevent the economy from slipping into deflation, with the special problems that entails.

As I have indicated, I believe that the combination of strong economic fundamentals and policymakers that are attentive to downside as well as upside risks to inflation make significant deflation in the United States in the foreseeable future quite unlikely. But suppose that, despite all precautions, deflation were to take hold in the U.S. economy and, moreover, that the Fed's policy instrument – the federal funds rate – were to fall to zero. What then? In the remainder of my talk I will discuss some possible options for stopping a deflation once it has gotten under way. I should emphasize that my comments on this topic are necessarily speculative, as the modern Federal Reserve has never faced this situation nor has it pre-committed itself formally to any specific course of action should deflation arise. Furthermore, the specific responses the Fed would undertake would presumably depend on a number of factors, including its assessment of the whole range of risks to the economy and any complementary policies being undertaken by other parts of the U.S. government.[7]

Curing Deflation

Let me start with some general observations about monetary policy at the zero bound, sweeping under the rug for the moment some technical and operational issues.

As I have mentioned, some observers have concluded that when the central bank's policy rate falls to zero – its practical minimum – monetary policy loses its ability to further stimulate aggregate demand and the economy. At a broad conceptual level, and in my view in practice as well, this conclusion is clearly mistaken. Indeed, under a fiat (that is, paper) money system, a government (in practice, the central bank in cooperation with other agencies) should always be able to generate increased nominal spending and inflation, even when the short-term nominal interest rate is at zero.

The conclusion that deflation is always reversible under a fiat money system follows from basic economic reasoning. A little parable may prove useful: Today an ounce of gold sells for $300, more or less. Now suppose that a modern alchemist solves his subject's oldest problem by finding a way to produce unlimited amounts of new gold at essentially no cost. Moreover, his invention is widely publicized and scientifically verified, and he announces his intention to begin massive production of gold within days. What would happen to the price of gold? Presumably, the potentially unlimited supply of cheap gold would cause the market price of gold to plummet. Indeed, if the market for gold is to any degree efficient, the price of gold would collapse immediately after the announcement of the invention, before the alchemist had produced and marketed a single ounce of yellow metal.

What has this got to do with monetary policy? Like gold, U.S. dollars have value only to the extent that they are strictly limited in supply. But the U.S. government has a technology, called a printing press (or, today, its electronic equivalent), that allows it to produce as many U.S. dollars as it wishes at essentially no cost. By increasing the number of U.S. dollars in circulation, or even by credibly threatening to do so, the U.S. government can also reduce the value of a dollar in terms of goods and services, which is equivalent to raising the prices in dollars of those goods and services. We conclude that, under a paper-money system, a determined government can always generate higher spending and hence positive inflation.

Of course, the U.S. government is not going to print money and distribute it willy-nilly (although as we will see later, there are practical policies that approximate this behavior).[8] Normally, money is injected into the economy through asset purchases by the Federal Reserve. To stimulate aggregate spending when short-term interest rates have reached zero, the Fed must expand the scale of its asset purchases or, possibly, expand the menu of assets that it buys. Alternatively, the Fed could find other ways of injecting money into the system – for example, by making low-interest-rate loans to banks or cooperating with the fiscal authorities. Each method of adding money to the economy has advantages and drawbacks, both technical and economic. One important concern in practice is that calibrating the economic effects of nonstandard means of injecting money may be difficult, given our relative lack of experience with such policies. Thus, as I have stressed already, prevention of deflation remains preferable to having to cure it. If we do fall into deflation, however, we can take comfort that the logic of the printing press example must assert itself, and sufficient injections of money will ultimately always reverse a deflation.

So what then might the Fed do if its target interest rate, the overnight federal funds rate, fell to zero? One relatively straightforward extension of current procedures would be to try to stimulate spending by lowering rates further out along the Treasury term structure – that is, rates on government bonds of longer maturities.[9] There are at least two ways of bringing down longer-term rates, which are complementary and could be employed separately or in combination. One approach, similar to an action taken in the past couple of years by the Bank of Japan, would be for the Fed to commit to holding the overnight rate at zero for some specified period. Because long-term interest rates represent averages of current and expected future short-term rates, plus a term premium, a commitment to keep short-term rates at zero for some time – if it were credible – would induce a decline in longer-term rates. A more direct method, which I personally prefer, would be for the Fed to begin announcing explicit ceilings for yields on longer-maturity Treasury debt (say, bonds maturing within the next two years). The Fed could enforce these interest-rate ceilings by committing to make unlimited purchases of securities up to two years from maturity at prices consistent with the targeted yields. If this program were successful, not only would yields on medium-term Treasury securities fall, but (because of links operating through expectations of future interest rates) yields on longer-term public and private debt (such as mortgages) would likely fall as well.

Lower rates over the maturity spectrum of public and private securities should strengthen aggregate demand in the usual ways and thus help to end deflation. Of course, if operating in relatively short-dated Treasury debt proved insufficient, the Fed could also attempt to cap yields of Treasury securities at still longer maturities, say three to six years. Yet another option would be for the Fed to use its existing authority to operate in the markets for agency debt (for example, mortgage-backed securities issued by Ginnie Mae, the Government National Mortgage Association).

Historical experience tends to support the proposition that a sufficiently determined Fed can peg or cap Treasury bond prices and yields at other than the shortest maturities. The most striking episode of bond-price pegging occurred during the years before the Federal Reserve-Treasury Accord of 1951.[10] Prior to that agreement, which freed the Fed from its responsibility to fix yields on government debt, the Fed maintained a ceiling of 2-1/2 percent on long-term Treasury bonds for nearly a decade. Moreover, it simultaneously established a ceiling on the twelve-month Treasury certificate of between 7/8 percent to 1-1/4 percent and, during the first half of that period, a rate of 3/8 percent on the 90-day Treasury bill. The Fed was able to achieve these low interest rates despite a level of outstanding government debt (relative to GDP) significantly greater than we have today, as well as inflation rates substantially more variable. At times, in order to enforce these low rates, the Fed had actually to purchase the bulk of outstanding 90-day bills. Interestingly, though, the Fed enforced the 2-1/2 percent ceiling on long-term bond yields for nearly a decade without ever holding a substantial share of long-maturity bonds outstanding.[11] For example, the Fed held 7.0 percent of outstanding Treasury securities in 1945 and 9.2 percent in 1951 (the year of the Accord), almost entirely in the form of 90-day bills. For comparison, in 2001 the Fed held 9.7 percent of the stock of outstanding Treasury debt.

To repeat, I suspect that operating on rates on longer-term Treasuries would provide sufficient leverage for the Fed to achieve its goals in most plausible scenarios. If lowering yields on longer-dated Treasury securities proved insufficient to restart spending, however, the Fed might next consider attempting to influence directly the yields on privately issued securities. Unlike some central banks, and barring changes to current law, the Fed is relatively restricted in its ability to buy private securities directly.[12] However, the Fed does have broad powers to lend to the private sector indirectly via banks, through the discount window.[13] Therefore a second policy option, complementary to operating in the markets for Treasury and agency debt, would be for the Fed to offer fixed-term loans to banks at low or zero interest, with a wide range of private assets (including, among others, corporate bonds, commercial paper, bank loans, and mortgages) deemed eligible as collateral.[14] For example, the Fed might make 90-day or 180-day zero-interest loans to banks, taking corporate commercial paper of the same maturity as collateral. Pursued aggressively, such a program could significantly reduce liquidity and term premiums on the assets used as collateral. Reductions in these premiums would lower the cost of capital both to banks and the nonbank private sector, over and above the beneficial effect already conferred by lower interest rates on government securities.[15]

The Fed can inject money into the economy in still other ways. For example, the Fed has the authority to buy foreign government debt, as well as domestic government debt. Potentially, this class of assets offers huge scope for Fed operations, as the quantity of foreign assets eligible for purchase by the Fed is several times the stock of U.S. government debt.[16]

I need to tread carefully here. Because the economy is a complex and interconnected system, Fed purchases of the liabilities of foreign governments have the potential to affect a number of financial markets, including the market for foreign exchange. In the United States, the Department of the Treasury, not the Federal Reserve, is the lead agency for making international economic policy, including policy toward the dollar; and the Secretary of the Treasury has expressed the view that the determination of the value of the U.S. dollar should be left to free market forces. Moreover, since the United States is a large, relatively closed economy, manipulating the exchange value of the dollar would not be a particularly desirable way to fight domestic deflation, particularly given the range of other options available. Thus, I want to be absolutely clear that I am today neither forecasting nor recommending any attempt by U.S. policymakers to target the international value of the dollar.

Although a policy of intervening to affect the exchange value of the dollar is nowhere on the horizon today, it's worth noting that there have been times when exchange rate policy has been an effective weapon against deflation. A striking example from U.S. history is Franklin Roosevelt's 40 percent devaluation of the dollar against gold in 1933-34, enforced by a program of gold purchases and domestic money creation. The devaluation and the rapid increase in money supply it permitted ended the U.S. deflation remarkably quickly. Indeed, consumer price inflation in the United States, year on year, went from -10.3 percent in 1932 to -5.1 percent in 1933 to 3.4 percent in 1934.[17] The economy grew strongly, and by the way, 1934 was one of the best years of the century for the stock market. If nothing else, the episode illustrates that monetary actions can have powerful effects on the economy, even when the nominal interest rate is at or near zero, as was the case at the time of Roosevelt's devaluation.

Fiscal Policy

Each of the policy options I have discussed so far involves the Fed's acting on its own. In practice, the effectiveness of anti-deflation policy could be significantly enhanced by cooperation between the monetary and fiscal authorities. A broad-based tax cut, for example, accommodated by a program of open-market purchases to alleviate any tendency for interest rates to increase, would almost certainly be an effective stimulant to consumption and hence to prices. Even if households decided not to increase consumption but instead re-balanced their portfolios by using their extra cash to acquire real and financial assets, the resulting increase in asset values would lower the cost of capital and improve the balance sheet positions of potential borrowers. A money-financed tax cut is essentially equivalent to Milton Friedman's famous "helicopter drop" of money.[18]

Of course, in lieu of tax cuts or increases in transfers the government could increase spending on current goods and services or even acquire existing real or financial assets. If the Treasury issued debt to purchase private assets and the Fed then purchased an equal amount of Treasury debt with newly created money, the whole operation would be the economic equivalent of direct open-market operations in private assets.

Japan

The claim that deflation can be ended by sufficiently strong action has no doubt led you to wonder, if that is the case, why has Japan not ended its deflation? The Japanese situation is a complex one that I cannot fully discuss today. I will just make two brief, general points.

First, as you know, Japan's economy faces some significant barriers to growth besides deflation, including massive financial problems in the banking and corporate sectors and a large overhang of government debt. Plausibly, private-sector financial problems have muted the effects of the monetary policies that have been tried in Japan, even as the heavy overhang of government debt has made Japanese policymakers more reluctant to use aggressive fiscal policies (for evidence see, for example, Posen, 1998). Fortunately, the U.S. economy does not share these problems, at least not to anything like the same degree, suggesting that anti-deflationary monetary and fiscal policies would be more potent here than they have been in Japan.

Second, and more important, I believe that, when all is said and done, the failure to end deflation in Japan does not necessarily reflect any technical infeasibility of achieving that goal. Rather, it is a byproduct of a longstanding political debate about how best to address Japan's overall economic problems. As the Japanese certainly realize, both restoring banks and corporations to solvency and implementing significant structural change are necessary for Japan's long-run economic health. But in the short run, comprehensive economic reform will likely impose large costs on many, for example, in the form of unemployment or bankruptcy. As a natural result, politicians, economists, businesspeople, and the general public in Japan have sharply disagreed about competing proposals for reform. In the resulting political deadlock, strong policy actions are discouraged, and cooperation among policymakers is difficult to achieve.

In short, Japan's deflation problem is real and serious; but, in my view, political constraints, rather than a lack of policy instruments, explain why its deflation has persisted for as long as it has. Thus, I do not view the Japanese experience as evidence against the general conclusion that U.S. policymakers have the tools they need to prevent, and, if necessary, to cure a deflationary recession in the United States.

Conclusion

Sustained deflation can be highly destructive to a modern economy and should be strongly resisted. Fortunately, for the foreseeable future, the chances of a serious deflation in the United States appear remote indeed, in large part because of our economy's underlying strengths but also because of the determination of the Federal Reserve and other U.S. policymakers to act preemptively against deflationary pressures. Moreover, as I have discussed today, a variety of policy responses are available should deflation appear to be taking hold. Because some of these alternative policy tools are relatively less familiar, they may raise practical problems of implementation and of calibration of their likely economic effects. For this reason, as I have emphasized, prevention of deflation is preferable to cure. Nevertheless, I hope to have persuaded you that the Federal Reserve and other economic policymakers would be far from helpless in the face of deflation, even should the federal funds rate hit its zero bound.[19]

References

- Ahearne, Alan, Joseph Gagnon, Jane Haltmaier, Steve Kamin, and others, "Preventing Deflation: Lessons from Japan's Experiences in the 1990s," Board of Governors, International Finance Discussion Paper No. 729, June 2002.
- Clouse, James, Dale Henderson, Athanasios Orphanides, David Small, and Peter Tinsley, "Monetary Policy When the Nominal Short-term Interest Rate Is Zero," Board of Governors of the Federal Reserve System, Finance and Economics Discussion Series No. 2000-51, November 2000.
- Eichengreen, Barry, and Peter M. Garber, "Before the Accord: U.S. Monetary-Financial Policy, 1945-51," in R. Glenn Hubbard,

ed., *Financial Markets and Financial Crises*, Chicago: University of Chicago Press for NBER, 1991.

- Eggertson, Gauti, "How to Fight Deflation in a Liquidity Trap: Committing to Being Irresponsible," unpublished paper, International Monetary Fund, October 2002.
- Fisher, Irving, "The Debt-Deflation Theory of Great Depressions," *Econometrica* (March 1933) pp. 337-57.
- Hetzel, Robert L. and Ralph F. Leach, "The Treasury-Fed Accord: A New Narrative Account," Federal Reserve Bank of Richmond, *Economic Quarterly* (Winter 2001) pp. 33-55.
- Orphanides, Athanasios and Volker Wieland, "Efficient Monetary Design Near Price Stability," *Journal of the Japanese and International Economies* (2000) pp. 327-65.
- Posen, Adam S., *Restoring Japan's Economic Growth*, Washington, D.C.: Institute for International Economics, 1998.
- Reifschneider, David, and John C. Williams, "Three Lessons for Monetary Policy in a Low-Inflation Era," *Journal of Money, Credit, and Banking* (November 2000) Part 2 pp. 936-66.
- Toma, Mark, "Interest Rate Controls: The United States in the 1940s," *Journal of Economic History* (September 1992) pp. 631-50.

Footnotes

1. Conceivably, deflation could also be caused by a sudden, large expansion in aggregate supply arising, for example, from rapid gains in productivity and broadly declining costs. I don't know of any unambiguous example of a supply-side deflation, although China in recent years is a possible case. Note that a supply-side deflation would be associated with an economic boom rather than a recession.

2. The nominal interest rate is the sum of the real interest rate and expected inflation. If expected inflation moves with actual inflation, and the real interest rate is not too variable, then the nominal interest rate declines when inflation declines – an effect known as the Fisher effect, after the early twentieth-century economist Irving Fisher. If the rate of deflation is equal to or greater than the real interest rate, the Fisher effect predicts that the nominal interest rate will equal zero.

3. The real interest rate equals the nominal interest rate minus the expected rate of inflation (see the previous footnote). The real interest rate measures the real (that is, inflation-adjusted) cost of borrowing or lending.

4. Throughout the latter part of the nineteenth century, a worldwide gold shortage was forcing down prices in all countries tied to the gold standard. Ironically, however, by the time that Bryan made his famous speech, a new cyanide-based method for extracting gold from ore had greatly increased world gold supplies, ending the deflationary pressure.

5. A rather different, but historically important, problem associated with the zero bound is the possibility that policymakers may mistakenly interpret the zero nominal interest rate as signaling conditions of "easy money." The Federal Reserve apparently made this error in the 1930s. In fact, when prices are falling, the real interest rate may be high and monetary policy tight, despite a nominal interest rate at or near zero.

6. Several studies have concluded that the measured rate of inflation overstates the "true" rate of inflation, because of several biases in standard price indexes that are difficult to eliminate in practice. The upward bias in the measurement of true inflation is another reason to aim for a measured inflation rate above zero.

7. See Clouse et al. (2000) for a more detailed discussion of monetary policy options when the nominal short-term interest rate is zero.

8. Keynes, however, once semi-seriously proposed, as an anti-deflationary measure, that the government fill bottles with currency and bury them in mine shafts to be dug up by the public.

9. Because the term structure is normally upward sloping, especially during periods of economic weakness, longer-term rates could be significantly above zero even when the overnight rate is at the zero bound.

10. S See Hetzel and Leach (2001) for a fascinating account of the events leading to the Accord.

11. See Eichengreen and Garber (1991) and Toma (1992) for descriptions and analyses of the pre-Accord period. Both articles conclude that the Fed's commitment to low inflation helped convince investors to hold long-term bonds at low rates in the 1940s and 1950s. (A similar dynamic would work in the Fed's favor today.) The rate-pegging policy finally collapsed because the money creation associated with buying Treasury securities was generating inflationary pressures. Of course, in a deflationary situation, generating inflationary pressure is precisely what the policy is trying to accomplish.

An episode apparently less favorable to the view that the Fed can manipulate Treasury yields was the so-called Operation Twist of the 1960s, during which an attempt was made to raise short-term yields and lower long-term yields simultaneously by selling at the short end and buying at the long end. Academic opinion on the effectiveness of Operation Twist is divided. In any case, this episode was rather small in scale, did not involve explicit announcement of target rates, and occurred when interest rates were not close to zero.

12. The Fed is allowed to buy certain short-term private instruments, such as bankers' acceptances, that are not much used today. It is also permitted to make IPC (individual, partnership, and corporation) loans directly to the private sector, but only under stringent criteria. This latter power has not been used since the Great Depression but could be invoked in an emergency deemed sufficiently serious by the Board of Governors.

13. Effective January 9, 2003, the discount window will be restructured into a so-called Lombard facility, from which well-capitalized banks will be able to borrow freely at a rate above the federal funds rate. These changes have no important bearing on the present discussion.

14. By statute, the Fed has considerable leeway to determine what assets to accept as collateral.

15. In carrying out normal discount window operations, the Fed absorbs virtually no credit risk because the borrowing bank remains responsible for repaying the discount window loan even if the issuer of the asset used as collateral defaults. Hence both the private issuer of the asset and the bank itself would have to fail nearly simultaneously for the Fed to take a loss. The fact that the Fed bears no credit risk places a limit on how far down the Fed can drive the cost of capital to private nonbank borrowers. For various reasons the Fed might well be reluctant to incur credit risk, as would happen if it bought assets directly from the private nonbank sector. However, should this additional measure become necessary, the Fed could of course always go to the Congress to ask for the requisite powers to buy private assets. The Fed also has emergency powers to make loans to the private sector (see footnote 12), which could be brought to bear if necessary.

16. The Fed has committed to the Congress that it will not use this power to "bail out" foreign governments; hence in practice it would purchase only highly rated foreign government debt.

17. U.S. Bureau of the Census, *Historical Statistics of the United States, Colonial Times to 1970*, Washington, D.C.: 1976.

18. A tax cut financed by money creation is the equivalent of a bond-financed tax cut plus an open-market operation in bonds by the Fed, and so arguably no explicit coordination is needed. However, a pledge by the Fed to keep the Treasury's borrowing costs low, as would be the case under my preferred alternative of fixing portions of the Treasury yield curve, might increase the willingness of the fiscal authorities to cut taxes.

Some have argued (on theoretical rather than empirical grounds) that a money-financed tax cut might not stimulate people to spend more because the public might fear that future tax increases will just "take back" the money they have received. Eggertson (2002) provides a theoretical analysis showing that, if government bonds are not indexed to inflation and certain other conditions apply, a money-financed tax cut will in fact raise spending and inflation. In brief, the reason is that people know that inflation erodes the real value of the government's debt and, therefore, that it is in the interest of the government to create some inflation. Hence they will believe the government's promise not to "take back" in future taxes the money distributed by means of the tax cut.

19. Some recent academic literature has warned of the possibility of an "uncontrolled deflationary spiral," in which deflation feeds on itself and becomes inevitably more severe. To the best of my knowledge, none of these analyses consider feasible policies of the type that I have described today. I have argued here that these policies would eliminate the possibility of uncontrollable deflation.

APPENDIX B

A Bernanke Bibliography

- Ben Bernanke (2005). *Essays on the Great Depression.* Princeton University Press. *ISBN 0-691-11820-5.*

- Ben Bernanke, Thomas Laubach, Frederic Mishkin, and Adam Posen (2005). *Inflation Targeting: Lessons from the International Experience.* Princeton University Press. *ISBN 0-691-08689-3.*

- Ben Bernanke and Alan Blinder (1992). "The Federal Funds Rate and the Channels of Monetary Transmission". *Economic Review* 82, no. 4: 901–921.

- Andrew B. Abel, Ben S. Bernanke (2001). *"Macroeconomics".* Addison Wesley. *ISBN 0-201-44133-0.*

- Ben S. Bernanke, Robert H. Frank (2007). *"Principles of Macro Economics".* McGraw Hill. ISBN-13: 978-0-07-319397-7.